# OF LIBERTY

## The Hidden History of Slavery, Four Presidents, and FIVE BLACK LIVES

### KENNETH C. DAVIS

HENRY HOLT AND COMPANY
NEW YORK

Henry Holt and Company
*Publishers since 1866*
175 Fifth Avenue, New York, New York 10010
MACKIDS.COM

Image sources (additional credits are noted with captions): p. ii: The White House Historical Association; p. iii: Unknown photographer / Tracy W. McGregor Library of American History, Special Collections, University of Virginia Library; pp.vi–vii: Library of Congress, Rare Book and Special Collections Division, LC-USZ62-44000; p. viii: National Gallery of Art, Washington; p. xvi: Library of Congress, Rare Book and Special Collections Division, ppmsca-19705; p. 9: National Portrait Gallery, Washington (Benjamin Franklin); United States Congress, senate.gov (Patrick Henry); p. 10: United States Congress, senate.gov (Henry Laurens); Schuyler Mansion State Historic Site, Albany (Philip Schuyler); Clark Art Institute, Williamstown, MA (George Washington); The White House Historical Association (Thomas Jefferson); p. 11: The White House Historical Association (James Madison); United States Congress, senate.gov (Andrew Jackson); p. 20: Wikimedia / "La Traite Rochelaise" Jean-Michel Deveau; p. 38–39: Wikimedia / Architect of the Capitol, aoc.gov; p. 71: Wikimedia / Jean-Baptiste-Antoine DeVerger; p. 95 : *The Pennsylvania Gazette*, Philadelphia, Pennsylvania; p. 101: Wikimedia / ephemeralnewyork.files.wordpress .com; p. 108: Wikimedia / John Fanning Watson, *Annals of Philadelphia* (1830); p. 180: Wikimedia / U.S. Navy Portrait; p. 197: Wikimedia / T. H. Welch, James Barton Longacre, picturehistory.com; p. 217: Wikimedia / Mathew Brady.

Library of Congress Cataloging-in-Publication Data
Names: Davis, Kenneth C.
Title: In the shadow of Liberty : the hidden history of slavery, four presidents, and five black lives / Kenneth C. Davis.
Description: First edition. | New York : Henry Holt and Company, 2016. | Audience: Ages 10 to 14. | Includes bibliographical references and index.
Identifiers: LCCN 2015035204 | ISBN 9781627793117 (hardcover : alkaline paper) | ISBN 9781627793124 (ebook)
Subjects: LCSH: Slaves—United States—Biography—Juvenile literature. | African Americans—Biography—Juvenile literature. | Presidents—Relations with African Americans—History—Juvenile literature. | Slavery—United States—History—Juvenile literature. | United States—Race relations—History—Juvenile literature. | BISAC: JUVENILE NONFICTION / People & Places / United States / African American. | JUVENILE NONFICTION / History / United States / Colonial & Revolutionary Periods.
Classification: LCC E444 .D36 2016 | DDC 920.0092/96073—dc23
LC record available at http://lccn.loc.gov/2015035204

Our books may be purchased in bulk for promotional, educational, or business use. Please contact your local bookseller or the Macmillan Corporate and Premium Sales Department at (800) 221-7945 ext. 5442 or by e-mail at MacmillanSpecialMarkets@macmillan.com.

First edition—2016 / Designed by Meredith Pratt
Printed in the United States of America by R. R. Donnelley & Sons Company, Harrisonburg, Virginia

1  3  5  7  9  10  8  6  4  2

To the devoted teachers and
librarians who help guide us
in our quest for truth

Store Room

# CONTENTS

# OUT OF THE

# SHADOWS

## WHO IS HE?

Standing in a 1796 portrait of the Washington family is a house servant in uniform, a black man in profile, his features vague and shadowy. The other figures are clearly shown: President George Washington and his wife, Martha, along with their grandchildren, Nelly and Wash Custis. We know that the map on the table shows the site of the nation's future capital city. But who is the black man in the shadows? Nobody knows for sure.

Most of us learn something about America's presidents. You may have their pictures on your classroom walls. They are certainly in your pockets and piggy banks: George Washington on the quarter and dollar bill, Thomas Jefferson on the nickel and rarely used two-dollar bill, and Andrew Jackson currently on the twenty. Across America, there are schools, cities, and other landmarks named in their honor.

But this book is about some people who are not famous.

They don't have towns or schools named after them. They are five enslaved people who were legally the "property" of some of America's most famous men. Like that mystery man in the background of the Washington family portrait, these enslaved people were hidden in the shadows of history.

They lived with these powerful men and their families every day, sometimes "24–7," as we like to say today. Each witnessed extraordinary events. And each has a story to tell about what being enslaved meant in early America:

- William "Billy" Lee and a young woman named Ona Judge were enslaved by George Washington. Billy Lee remained with Washington all of his life. Ona Judge escaped her bondage, bravely challenging America's most powerful man.

- Isaac Granger grew up on Thomas Jefferson's plantation during the American Revolution and lived among the enslaved people who were called "family" by the author of the Declaration of Independence.

- Paul Jennings was born enslaved and taken as a young boy to the White House by James Madison. He watched the city of Washington burn during the War of 1812 and stood beside the deathbed of the man called the Father of the Constitution.

- Alfred Jackson grew up the son of an enslaved cook at the Hermitage, Andrew Jackson's Tennessee plantation. He survived the Civil War, lived into the twentieth century, and is buried in the family garden near the seventh president and his wife.

Because these five people were "owned" by men considered great presidents, we know their names and parts of their stories. Luckily, because of their connections to these presidents, there are records to help us understand who they were and how they lived. These five lives help show us an important part of the great tragedy and complexity of American slavery. In a way, these five stories are as important as accounts of the men who were their legal "masters."

America ended legal slavery more than 150 years ago, after four years of a catastrophic civil war that took the lives of as many as 750,000 Americans, according to new estimates. We may learn something about slavery in school. But many people still do not understand or want to accept this basic truth: America was "conceived in liberty" in 1776, but the country was also born in shackles. Africans stolen from their homes were brought to America before the Pilgrims arrived on the *Mayflower.* From the country's earliest days, slavery was an undeniable fact of American life.

This book is about how the threads of slavery were woven deeply into almost every aspect of American society for centuries. It is about how important slavery was to the nation's birth and growth and to the men who led the country for so long. It is about wealth and political power and untold misery.

It is also about the deep scars that slavery left on America—old wounds that surface in racial conflict today. Some people believe that slavery is ancient history, a thing of the past that no longer matters. That is wrong. "The past is never dead," wrote the American novelist William Faulkner, a son of the South. "It's not even past."

And that is especially true of America's slave past.

For more than two hundred years, racial slavery was as much a part of our nation's story as Pilgrims, presidents, pioneers, wagons rolling west, and waves of immigrants streaming to America's shores. Well into the twentieth century and the civil rights movement, the poisonous legacy of slavery shaped many attitudes about African Americans.

For much of that time—in letters, newspapers, books, and speeches—many white people commonly described enslaved African Americans as shiftless or lazy, disrespectful or "uppity," and ignorant. Often compared to apes and monkeys, they were thought dangerous—especially young black men. Those cruel and wrong stereotypes eventually became attitudes widely accepted by generations of Americans, white and black. Those prejudices continue to the present day.

More important, slavery destroyed society's most basic pillar—the family. It did so by telling enslaved people if and when they could marry. It made marriage a whim of the master rather than a legal right. It made women sexual slaves whose children were slaves. And it tore mothers from children and wives from their husbands, to be sold for profit or punishment.

In many years of writing about American history, I have tried to answer a hard but crucial question. It has to do with the gaping hole between the words and deeds of many of America's great men. These men fought for independence and were true believers in concepts like liberty and equality. How could such men keep other human beings as slaves, denying their freedom and basic rights?

Before writing this book, I tried to answer that question by looking at the writings and actions of Washington, Jefferson, and other men known as the Founding Fathers. But now I want to answer in a different way—by learning about the lives of some people who were enslaved by four of America's greatest heroes.

For generations, American history books hid or downplayed the evils of slavery. Many presidential biographers were willing to gaze past the cruelty that was central to slavery, along with the key role it played in the lives of some presidents. Young children learned about George Washington's honesty in a fictitious story of a cherry tree. But most students heard little about the hundreds of people forced to labor in Washington's house and fields, or the enslaved men who fought America's wars and built the White House.

There is no way to gloss over slavery. It was a murderous crime against humanity. Its brutal tools were whips, manacles, and floating prisons called slave ships. Its unspeakable methods included beatings, rape, and murder. It relied on a racist belief that white people were superior to black people—a concept based on ancient religious teachings and tainted scientific notions. Many historians argue that American racism—the belief in white racial superiority—did not exist until it grew out of slavery.

Slavery always relied on ignorance—keeping the enslaved from learning to read or write because books and words carry the ideas that help set people free. Ignorance of the ABCs, Frederick Douglass would write after gaining his freedom, was part of "the white man's power to enslave the black man." As he recorded in his autobiography, "I set out with high hope, and a fixed purpose, at whatever cost of trouble, to learn how to read."

Today, it is ignorance of slavery that must be fixed. Slavery can no longer be treated like an embarrassing relative whose face is cropped out of a family photo. Trying to avoid the shame of slavery once led historians to cover it up. Many of the facts linking some of America's greatest men with the basic evil of slavery have been swept under the carpet.

But as John Adams, another Founding Father, once said, "Facts are stubborn things."

This book is about some stubborn facts. They are not fun or pretty.

The history we learn is often about dates, battles, famous speeches, and court decisions. And it is important to understand those. But in the end, history is not just about wars and constitutional amendments, facts we memorize. It is about people. This book tells the real story of real people—all of them born in slavery's shackles—who were considered the property of some American heroes.

It is a story we all need to understand. And that is how we can bring their faces and lives out of the shadows. Only then can we understand what slavery once meant to this country— and to the people who lived in slavery and to those who kept them. Only then can we really understand and possibly move past the stain of a racist past that still haunts America.

# NOTE TO THE READER

The way we use words to label people and identify things is important. In this book, I use the term *enslaved person* instead of *slave* when referring to individuals who, under the laws of the day, were the legal property of other people. It is very different to say, for example, that "William Lee was born enslaved" than it is to say, "William Lee was Washington's slave." This critical distinction reflects how we think about the people who were victims trapped in a powerful system. To say that people were *enslaved* means this condition was forced on them; it does not define who they were. It is meant as a respectful term for the individuality of the enslaved people.

Throughout this book, the actual words of formerly enslaved people are sometimes used as they were recorded many years ago. Often their words were set down in a style that attempted to capture the original regional dialect and grammar. That not only can be confusing to today's readers but sometimes makes the speaker appear ignorant. I have occasionally used modern spellings to clarify the meaning of these personal accounts and recollections. For instance, if a person had once said "'belled," that has been changed to "rebelled," and the word "Massa" appears as "Master." This was done only to make the words and experiences of these people clear.

# IN THE
# SHADOW
# ★ LIBERTY
OF

# CHAPTER ONE

# "THE LOUDEST YELPS

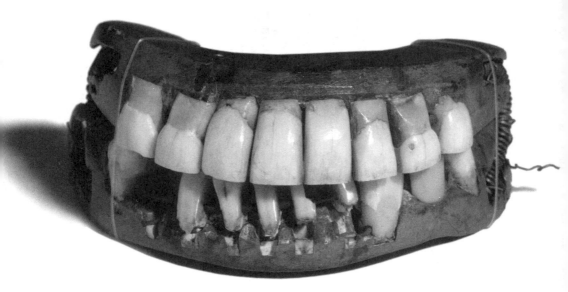

*The only remaining full set of Washington's dentures.*
[Mount Vernon Ladies' Association]

# FOR LIBERTY"

How is it that we hear the loudest yelps for liberty
among the drivers of negroes?
—Dr. Samuel Johnson, *Taxation No Tyranny*, 1775

The time is now near at hand which must
probably determine, whether Americans are
to be, Freemen, or Slaves.
—George Washington, July 2, 1776

Maybe you've heard that George Washington had wooden teeth. That's false—an old legend. Nobody is even sure how it got started.

It is true that Washington lost most of his own teeth, which was hardly unusual in the days before modern dentists and fluoride toothpaste. Over the years, Washington owned several sets of false teeth. But they were not carved from wood. Washington's dentures were actually made from lead, ivory, bone, and animal teeth. Some of them were made with human teeth.

That idea may seem strange enough. But what if some of those human teeth belonged to enslaved people on Washington's plantation?

George Washington had teeth yanked from the mouths of his enslaved people, records show, which may have then been transplanted into Washington's dentures or even his jaw. Washington paid for nine teeth—a total of 122 shillings (about $755 in today's dollars), to be exact. That idea may seem gross today. But back then it was entirely normal for wealthy people to buy teeth from the poor.

George Washington was eleven years old when his father died. The future president inherited one of his father's farms and, with it, ten enslaved people. Later, as an ambitious farmer, George Washington relied completely on enslaved labor to grow his crops, catch fish in the nearby Potomac River, clean his house, make his clothes, and put food on his table. Long before the American Revolution, Washington was eager to add more enslaved workers, especially if he could strike a bargain. And that was what happened in October 1767.

Thirty-five-year-old George Washington was riding through his home county in colonial Virginia when he stopped to take part in an estate sale. One of Washington's neighbors, Colonel

John Lee, had died, and his property was being auctioned to pay off the dead man's debts. That estate included all of the enslaved people on the plantation.

The future war hero and president successfully bid on two "mulatto" brothers, named Frank and Will Lee. (Their story is told in Chapter Three.) At the same auction, Washington also bought Adam and Jack, two "Negro boys."

In a time before there were bank checks or credit cards, Washington made this deal with a written note promising to pay eighteen months later. One of Virginia's most prominent men, Washington had only to give his word. That was enough

*In this depiction of a slave auction circa 1849, a mother begs to keep her baby from being taken from her.* [Manuscripts and Rare Books Division, Schomburg Center for Research in Black Culture, The New York Public Library, Astor, Lenox and Tilden Foundations]

to make these four boys his personal property. Precise about keeping track of matters that related to his plantation, he recorded the details in an account book:

| | |
|---|---|
| Mulatto Will | £61-15 |
| Ditto Frank | 50 |
| Negro boy Adam | 19 |
| Jack | 19 |
| | £149-15-0 |

The symbol £ stands for British pounds, the currency used at the time in colonial Virginia. £61-15 meant 61 pounds and 15 shillings.

Washington was able to buy the two "Negro" boys at a much lower price than he paid for Frank and Will Lee because they were destined for Washington's fields, where he grew tobacco, corn, wheat, and other crops. Washington paid more than three times as much for "Mulatto Will" and Frank since he planned to train the two brothers to become personal attendants in his Mount Vernon home.

Why? To modern ears, it sounds strange. But Frank and Will were known at the time as "yellow skinned." Light-skinned enslaved people were prized simply because they looked more white. Many white slaveholders, especially in Virginia's upper-class homes, considered mixed-race people a sort of status symbol, just as some people today think of a flashy car or an expensive new smartphone. Washington and other white people used the word *mulatto* for such mixed-race people. The word may come from the Spanish word for a mule, an animal that is a cross between a horse and a donkey.

In time, Frank Lee learned to be Washington's head butler. William Lee, about sixteen years old at the time of the auction, became George Washington's valet, or personal servant. Called Will or Billy, he accompanied George Washington nearly every day of his life, tending to all his daily needs.

When George Washington purchased Billy, Frank, and the other two boys in 1767, Virginia was one of thirteen British colonies in America. The push for independence was still nearly ten years away, and George Washington was not thinking about going to war for America's freedom. As a loyal British citizen, Washington had fought for Great Britain's king and become a hero in the French and Indian War in America (part of Europe's later Seven Years' War).

But by 1775, Washington was no longer a happy British subject. Like other Americans, he complained that British taxes on printed paper and other goods were unfair and that other British laws were a form of tyranny. Some Americans even claimed that these taxes and the way the colonists were treated amounted to a form of slavery. Their protests set the American colonies on the path to freedom.

As the angry American objections turned into boycotts of British imports like paper and tea, a famous Englishman named Dr. Samuel Johnson wrote a short pamphlet called *Taxation No Tyranny*. In it, Dr. Johnson asked, "How is it that we hear the loudest yelps for liberty among the drivers of negroes?"

A yelp is the short, sharp cry or bark of a dog. When Dr. Johnson wrote that, the word *yelp* was sometimes used to describe the barks of bloodhounds that tracked runaway slaves. Dr. Johnson was mocking Americans who wanted it both ways—they complained about taxes they considered unjust, but at the same time, many of them owned or traded slaves. This pamphlet appeared in 1775, a few months before the first shots in the American Revolution were fired at Lexington and Concord in Massachusetts on April 19, 1775.

*Dr. Samuel Johnson, painted here by Joshua Reynolds, made fun of Americans who complained about their freedom while owning and trading enslaved people.* [Library of Congress, Prints & Photographs Division, LC-DIG-det-4a26286]

Dr. Johnson's simple question gets to the heart of a basic and uncomfortable fact: some of the rowdiest cries for America's freedom came from the Founding Fathers, heroes in the American quest for liberty. The list of Founding Fathers who owned enslaved people or profited in some way from slavery is long and filled with both familiar and less famous names.

**BENJAMIN FRANKLIN** owned enslaved people—although he called them servants. He later changed his mind and led one of the first societies aimed at abolishing slavery, in 1790.

**PATRICK HENRY,** the Virginia politician famed for his words "give me liberty, or give me death," did not think his enslaved servants deserved the same deal. While Patrick Henry thought slavery was "repugnant," he never freed any enslaved people because of the "general inconveniency of living without them."

**HENRY LAURENS** of South Carolina, the president of the Continental Congress for a term, had become one of America's richest men by shipping as many as 8,000 people from Africa to America.

**PHILIP SCHUYLER,** a patriot leader and general in the American Revolution, was among New York's wealthiest men. More than twenty-five enslaved people labored in his home, fields, and mills in upstate New York. Yes, there was slavery in New York—and all of the other original thirteen states, North and South.

Of course, the two men most closely connected with America's fight for freedom—

**GEORGE WASHINGTON** and **THOMAS JEFFERSON,** chief author of the Declaration of

Independence—bought, sold, and owned hundreds of human beings.

**JAMES MADISON,** the fourth American president, was also a slaveholder. During the summer of 1787, he was one of the men who helped create the United States Constitution, which called for a "more perfect union" to "promote the Blessings of Liberty." Madison's many enslaved people could not enjoy those blessings.

**ANDREW JACKSON,** the hero of the War of 1812, once said, "The individual who refuses to defend his rights, when called upon by his government, deserves to be a slave." Andrew Jackson had more than one hundred enslaved people on his plantation when he became the seventh president.

Four presidents—Washington, Jefferson, Madison, and Jackson. Each man a hero of America's birth and early years. Each fought for freedom. Each is remembered with monuments, memorials, and cities named in his honor. Their stately homes—Mount Vernon, Monticello, Montpelier, and the Hermitage—are major tourist attractions. And all of them are viewed as great leaders in the quest for liberty, the rule of law, and basic rights.

Along with James Monroe, the fifth president, these men held office for forty of the first forty-eight years of the American presidency. All were slaveholders. Of the first seven U.S. presidents, only John Adams, the second president, and his son, John Quincy Adams, the sixth president, never owned any slaves. They thought slavery was wrong.

In fact, before Abraham Lincoln was elected in 1860, ten of the first fifteen American presidents owned enslaved people or grew up in slaveholding households. Until 1850, many of these presidents brought enslaved servants to work at the White House, which was also built and maintained with enslaved labor.

The people who were legal "property" of presidents were among the millions of enslaved people who lived and toiled in America—and who were stuck in the shadows, too. Their stories begin long before America was born, with the arrival of the first Africans brought to American shores in chains.

# THIRTEEN
# AMERICAN PRESIDENTS

owned enslaved people or were raised
in slaveholding households:

George Washington

Thomas Jefferson

James Madison

James Monroe

Andrew Jackson

Martin Van Buren

William Henry Harrison

John Tyler

James K. Polk

Zachary Taylor

Andrew Johnson

Ulysses S. Grant

Woodrow Wilson

Martin Van Buren's father kept six slaves in his Kinderhook, New York, tavern. In the case of Grant, his enslaved people were given to his wife by his father-in-law.

The last president to grow up in a slaveholding household was Woodrow Wilson, who became the twenty-eighth president in 1913. He was born in Virginia in 1856, before the Civil War began.

# SLAVERY IN AMERICA TIME LINE
## 1492–1700

**1492** — Columbus makes the first of four voyages to the "New World." Black men arrive with Columbus as sailors, and other Africans come as soldiers with the Spanish explorers who later conquer and colonize the Caribbean islands and the Americas.

**AUGUST 20, 1619** — Twenty Africans are brought to the English colony of Jamestown, Virginia. Sold as indentured servants, these African captives must work for a period of time but are promised their freedom. Although not the first Africans in North America, they are considered the first Africans to settle in the future United States.

**1624** — The Dutch colony of New Amsterdam (later New York) is founded by approximately 100 settlers; within a year, as many as eleven black African male slaves arrive from Angola.

**1638** — The first American ship carrying enslaved Africans from the Caribbean island of Barbados, the *Desire,* sails into Boston Harbor; its cargo also includes salt, cotton, and tobacco.

**1645** — The *Rainbow*, the first American ship bound for Africa to trade for captives and return them to America, sails from Boston.

**1652** — Rhode Island, a New England colony, outlaws slavery. But the slave trade becomes so profitable that slavery is later permitted; Newport, Rhode Island, emerges as a major slave port.

**1662** — A Virginia law declares that children take on the status of their mothers. Under this law, children born of enslaved mothers are also enslaved, even if their father is white and free.

| **1664** | The British establish legal slavery when they take over the colonies of New York and New Jersey. Maryland passes a similar law, which also states that freeborn women who marry enslaved men are considered enslaved. |
| **1684** | Africans are imported into Philadelphia, beginning a thriving slave trade in that city. |
| **1688** | In Germantown, near Philadelphia, four Quakers issue what is considered the first American antislavery petition. Based on the Golden Rule, "Do unto others as you would have them do unto you," the petition asks fellow Quakers to give up their slaves. |
| **1694** | South Carolina begins to grow rice; a boom in rice farming creates an increased demand for slave labor. |
| **1700** | In Boston, Judge Samuel Sewall, one of the judges in the famous Salem witch trials, writes one of the first antislavery tracts in America. In *The Selling of Joseph*, he writes, "All Men, as they are the Sons of *Adam* . . . have equal Right unto Liberty." |

By 1700, there are approximately 28,000 black people in British North America, about 11 percent of the total population, then estimated around 250,000. Enslaved people are being imported into Virginia at the rate of about 1,000 per year.

The African slave trade becomes the world's most profitable business during the eighteenth century.

# CHAPTER TWO

# STOLEN

# FROM AFRICA

If slavery be wrong, it is justified by the example of all the world. . . . In all ages one half of mankind have been slaves.
—CHARLES PINCKNEY,
DELEGATE TO THE CONSTITUTIONAL CONVENTION, 1787

When I looked round the ship too and saw a large furnace of copper boiling, and a multitude of black people of every description chained together, every one of their countenances expressing dejection and sorrow, I no longer doubted of my fate; and, quite overpowered with horror and anguish, I fell motionless on the deck and fainted. When I recovered a little, I found some black people about me. . . . I asked them if we were not to be eaten by those white men with horrible looks, red faces, and long hair.
—*THE INTERESTING NARRATIVE OF THE LIFE OF OLAUDAH EQUIANO, OR GUSTAVUS VASSA, THE AFRICAN,* 1789

*A depiction of enslaved Africans aboard the* Wildfire *circa 1860.*
[Library of Congress, Prints & Photographs Division, LC-USZ62-19607]

The boy sat in a tree, high above the African jungle. While the adults were working in nearby fields, it was his job to call out a warning if dangerous animals or strangers approached. Once, he saw a man sneak into the village and try to take some children. Raising the alarm, the boy yelled at the top of his lungs until the village adults came. They caught the stranger and tied him up. Everyone in this African village was safe for the day.

The next time, the boy—no more than ten years old—was not so lucky.

"One day, when all our people were gone out to their works as usual, and only I and my dear sister were left to mind the house," he later recalled, "two men and a woman got over our walls, and in a moment seized us both, and, without giving us time to cry out, or make resistance, they stopped our mouths, and ran off with us into the nearest wood."

No alarm was raised this time. The strangers gagged both children, tied them up, and bundled them away before anyone knew they were gone.

Kidnapped!

After a few days' travel, the boy was sold as a servant to another village. Separated from his sister, he didn't know if he would ever see her or the rest of his family again. Although he was treated fairly well by his masters, the small boy had only one wish—to return home.

*A group of captive Africans are taken to a slave ship by Arab traders in an illustration by Frederic Shoberl, published in* The World in Miniature: Africa *(1821).* [Library of Virginia]

Then, while tending chickens one day, he killed one by accident. Afraid of being punished, he ran away. When caught, he was sold again. The men who took him carried him farther and farther away from his home. Moving through one strange village after another, the boy no longer understood the languages he heard.

Eventually, the boy was taken to the seacoast and sold yet again. Nearly six months had passed since he had been

*The* Rochelle, *a French slave ship, circa 1741.*

snatched from his village. After being traded once more, he was brought aboard a large, strange ship riding at anchor.

"I was soon put down under the decks, and there I received such a salutation in my nostrils as I had never experienced in my life," the boy recalled. "With the loathsomeness of the stench . . . I became so sick and low that I was not able to eat. . . . I now wished for the last friend, death, to relieve me; but soon, to my grief, two of the white men offered me eatables; and, on my refusing to eat, one of them held me fast by the hands, and laid me across I think the windlass, and tied my feet, while the other flogged me severely."

It is hard to imagine the terror experienced by a small boy caught like this, sometime in the 1750s. The man who later told that story was Olaudah Equiano, who also went by the name Gustavus Vassa.

But the nightmare was just beginning for him and the other kidnapped Africans forced belowdecks. Descending a ladder, they were assaulted by the stench of human waste and death. Next, they had to survive the trip across the Atlantic, the voyage known as the Middle Passage—the longest of three legs in the so-called Triangle Trade in which the first leg was European goods carried to Africa and exchanged for captives. After bringing slaves to the Americas, the last leg saw the ships return to Europe with raw materials or finished products, such as rum and molasses.

During the Middle Passage, the captives were all chained and pressed tightly together into a hellish space. Usually, they had no more than eighteen inches—barely room to turn over—above them. It was like being forced into a coffin. Many did not survive the journey.

In this floating death box, the transatlantic journey took from six to ten weeks. Food for the captives was scarce. Sometimes local items were available while the ships continued to trade along the African coast until the holds were filled with human cargo. During the long voyage, the meal offered to captives was usually little more than a worm-ridden gruel—a thin, watery boiled cereal—or a concoction called "dab-a-dab," a mash of beans, rice, and corn.

Sometimes, the desperate people in chains tried to strike back at the outnumbered crew. Resistance was futile. The white men had all the guns, whips, and swords. Locked together—frightened, weak, sick—many died from disease or starvation. The dead bodies were tossed overboard. Sharks followed the slave ships and attacked these bodies in a feeding frenzy that left the sea churning with blood.

Captains used the terror aroused by the ever-present sharks to enforce order. To strike fear among the captives, some captains would tie a woman with rope and lower her into the water. Her fellow captives would see the half-eaten remains of the victim raised from the ocean as a gruesome lesson in obedience. The cruel, sadistic methods of the slavers had one goal—to keep the captives alive but disciplined.

When this frightful journey from Africa's west coast was over, the survivors were usually delivered to the islands of Jamaica and Barbados or to Brazil, in South America. Before the captives were off-loaded, the crew would clean them. Like farm animals being prepared for judging at a county fair, the captives were made to look healthy. Ointments were applied to the oozing sores left by the tight shackles. Hair was darkened—gray hair or any other signs of age would reduce the value of the captive. Bodies were oiled to make them appear healthier.

All that mattered was fetching a good price for their human cargo in "the scramble." That was the rush of buyers to grab the best of the newly arrived captives. Every one of the chained prisoners was crudely inspected. Men's muscles—in their backs, arms, legs—were prodded and poked, tested for strength. For women, it meant checking their bodies, including their breasts and teeth, and posture. All sense of modesty or innocence was stripped away. Some were taken away to be "seasoned," trained in a slave's duties. Others were sent on to ships sailing for the slave ports of colonial America.

After spending nearly twenty years in slavery in America, Olaudah Equiano was able to purchase his freedom and later wrote an autobiography, *The Interesting Narrative of the Life of*

*Olaudah Equiano, or Gustavus Vassa, the African.* Published in London in 1789, his memoir told of being captured, carried across the ocean to Barbados, and sold to a merchant sea captain. His book was one of the first accounts by a former enslaved person ever published.

Although a few historians have recently cast doubt on some of the details of Olaudah Equiano's life story, the majority of his account has been verified. His depiction of the horrors of being stolen from his village, his captivity on the ship, the Middle Passage, and his life among the enslaved was a true picture. The same, and much worse, had happened to millions of people stolen from Africa.

His story also helped change people's minds. In England, Equiano's book created a wave of public opposition to slavery. It helped lead to passage of the law that abolished the British slave trade in 1807.

By the time Equiano published his book, slave ships had carried more than 160,000 Africans to America's Chesapeake colonies, 140,000 to the Carolinas and Georgia, and 30,000 to the northern colonies. Some 330,000 enslaved people were brought to the future United States of America, starting in the earliest colonial days to 1775, just before the American Revolution.

These numbers were a small fraction of the millions of Africans stolen and brutally shipped to Spanish, Dutch, French,

*A portrait of Olaudah Equiano, or Gustavus Vassa, whose published story helped launch the abolition movement.* [Library of Congress, Prints & Photographs Division, LC-USZ62-54026]

and British colonies in the Caribbean—especially Jamaica and Barbados—and the more than two million carried to the Portuguese colony of Brazil, where sugar plantations required vast numbers of workers.

The multitudes of Africans violently wrenched from their families and villages in this murderous global business is mind-boggling.

According to the best estimates, during the almost four hundred years of the African slave trade from the late fifteenth into the nineteenth century, 12.4 million people were loaded onto slave ships and carried across the Atlantic. "Along the dreadful way, 1.8 million of them died," historian Marcus Rediker recorded, "their bodies cast overboard to the sharks that followed the ships. Most of the 10.6 million who survived were thrown into the bloody maw of a killing plantation system."

The catastrophic death toll in the New World was part of a profitable system that was far from unique. Slavery is as old as humanity. It was an ancient and global practice that continues in parts of the world today as boys and girls continue to be sold into forced labor.

For many years, the notion that slavery had always been practiced—and, more important, approved by the Bible—was used by many Americans to defend slavery. Charles Pinckney of South Carolina, one of the delegates at the Constitutional Convention in 1787, said, "If slavery be wrong, it is justified by the example of the world. . . . In all ages one half of mankind have been slaves."

Throughout world history, slavery has taken on many forms, existing among the earliest societies. All the so-called great civilizations functioned with slavery in different forms. Ancient Egypt, Greece, and Rome had some type of slavery, usually based on the captivity of people conquered in wars. Long before Europeans came to the Americas, native nations such as the Aztec and Inca enslaved people, too.

The use of forced slave labor by Europeans began almost as soon as the first Spanish settlers arrived in the New World. The first groups that Europeans enslaved in the Americas were not Africans but the people called "Indians" by Columbus. They were forced to work in Spanish mines and large plantations in the Americas. Armed with guns, steel swords, and dogs wearing armor and spiked collars, the Spanish quickly conquered native people such as the Carib, Arawak, and Inca and forced them to dig for gold and silver and work on large estates. It was prison labor under threat of constant violence. A native who failed to bring enough gold out of a mine might have a hand chopped off. Spanish treasure galleons were soon sailing home loaded with riches from mines in Mexico and Peru. The Spanish built a global golden empire on these treasures, certain that Heaven had blessed them.

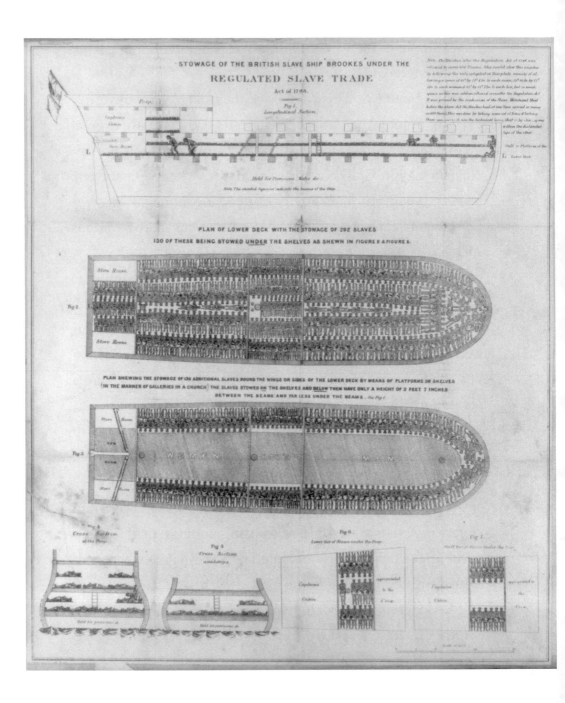

STOWAGE OF THE BRITISH SLAVE SHIP 'BROOKES' UNDER THE
REGULATED SLAVE TRADE
Act of 1788.

Fig 1.
Longitudinal Section.

PLAN OF LOWER DECK WITH THE STOWAGE OF 292 SLAVES
130 OF THESE BEING STOWED UNDER THE SHELVES AS SHEWN IN FIGURE 2 & FIGURE 3.

Fig 2.

PLAN SHEWING THE STOWAGE OF 130 ADDITIONAL SLAVES ROUND THE WINGS OR SIDES OF THE LOWER DECK BY MEANS OF PLATFORMS OR SHELVES
(IN THE MANNER OF GALLERIES IN A CHURCH) THE SLAVES STOWED ON THE SHELVES AND BELOW THEM HAVE ONLY A HEIGHT OF 2 FEET 7 INCHES
BETWEEN THE BEAMS AND FAR LESS UNDER THE BEAMS — See Fig 1.

Fig 3.

WOMEN                           MEN

The natives, of course, were not so fortunate. They were quickly dying. One reason was the harsh labor conditions. But another was an invisible killer: the Spanish and other European explorers brought deadly contagious diseases, like smallpox, to the Americas. Native people had little natural resistance, or immunity, to these new diseases. No one knows exactly how many native people died after Europeans arrived in the New World, but the estimated percentages are staggering—epidemics wiped out as many as 90 percent of some native communities.

When a Spanish priest saw how cruelly the natives were treated and how rapidly they were dying, he recommended a solution. This priest, Bartolomé de las Casas, suggested using imported African laborers instead of oppressing the native people. In 1518, the Spanish government created a system that licensed slave traders to bring Africans to the New World. This solution merely exchanged one deadly system for another.

As the Spanish and other European colonizers of the New World switched from a frenzied hunt for gold and silver to the production of cash crops like tobacco, rice, and sugar, the demand for African workers exploded. Wherever Europeans arrived to set up New World colonies—from Canada down to

*Published in 1788, this illustration of the British slave ship* Brookes *showed how tightly the captives were packed and was widely used by abolitionists to attack the slave trade.* [Library of Congress, Rare Book and Special Collections Division, LC-USZ62-44000]

Chile and Peru and across the Caribbean—slavery became key to the conquest of the Americas.

In later times, coal and oil would drive the great engines of American progress. They were the fuel that powered the railroads, factories, and machinery of the Industrial Age. But in early America, racial slavery powered progress. It made the system work and created great fortunes. Slavery was not a sideshow to the settlement and development of America but a central feature.

The first shipload of captive Africans to arrive in the future United States came to Jamestown, Virginia—the first permanent English settlement in America—in August 1619. John Rolfe, famed for his role in making tobacco a successful cash crop in Virginia and later marrying the woman known as Pocahontas, recorded that "20 and odd" Africans were brought to the settlement. Recent research suggests they may have been taken from Angola by Portuguese slave traders and then captured at sea by British pirates flying the Dutch flag, who then sold them in Virginia.

These Africans were actually purchased as "indentured servants" rather than slaves. An indentured servant was typically someone who agreed to work for several years in exchange for his or her passage, eventual freedom, and the promise of some land. In colonial America, both white and black people came as indentured servants, including some of those who sailed aboard the *Mayflower*.

After their period of indenture was over, they were released, if they were still alive. The death rate among indentured servants in colonial America was very high. Malnutrition, lack of medical care, diseases like malaria and yellow fever, harsh working conditions, severe punishments, and wars with local native people all took a heavy toll.

Some indentured servants came by choice. But many of those shipped to America were kidnapped children, orphans, and convicted criminals—meaning they had no say in the matter. For many years, indentured servants filled America's need for workers. By the 1630s, most people in colonial Virginia—whether they had chosen their life or not—were indentured servants.

Then something changed. By the early 1700s, fewer white Europeans were willing to accept the hardships of servitude in America. Frightening tales of death, disease, and the threat of "savage Indians" made many unwilling to risk the long ocean crossing and uncertain future. In European countries, the quality of life was also rapidly improving. Fewer wars and better sanitation and medical practices meant higher living standards. As conditions improved, fewer Europeans were willing to take the gamble of a servant's life in America.

But the American demand for field workers and household servants surged, especially in places like South Carolina, where rice production was booming. Along with sugar and tobacco, rice demands intense, backbreaking labor. The planters needed more slaves.

African slavery in America grew quickly because enslaved people were cheaper to buy than white servants. Africans were also thought to be physically strong and capable team workers. Accustomed to cooperative agriculture in which whole villages often farmed together, many Africans were used to working in large groups, the most efficient method for large American plantations. And many Europeans and Americans thought—incorrectly—that Africans were less likely to die from tropical diseases since they came from a tropical climate.

Because of their skin color and because few Africans spoke English, it was far more difficult for them to run away and mix into society, unlike white servants. Enslaved American Indians had been able to escape more easily since they were usually familiar with the local area and could return to their own people.

But one fact stood above all: Africans were enslaved for life. Unlike indentured servants who might eventually be freed, a slave was a slave forever—unless freed for some reason by an owner. All of these factors made the African slave trade a booming international business in the early 1700s.

By 1776, when Thomas Jefferson wrote the Declaration of Independence, there were 500,000 African Americans enslaved among the 2.5 million people in the thirteen colonies.

That great year of independence for America was a little less than ten years after George Washington purchased four boys named Jack, Adam, William, and Frank.

# SLAVERY IN AMERICA TIME LINE
## 1705–1776

**1705** Massachusetts declares marriage between whites and blacks illegal. Virginia rules that slaves are "real estate," restricts their travel, and calls for stricter penalties for marriage or sexual relations between the races, which had been illegal since 1691.

**1713** Quaker opposition to slavery in Philadelphia continues to grow; some Quakers develop a plan for emancipating slaves and returning them to their native lands in Africa.

**1739** The Stono Rebellion, a violent slave uprising, is put down in South Carolina. Thirty white people and forty-four black people die in the violence.

**1754** John Woolman, a Philadelphia Quaker and tailor, publishes *Some Considerations on the Keeping of Negroes: Recommended to the Professors of Christianity of Every Denomination.* Arguing that slavery is unchristian and cruel, it becomes the most widely distributed antislavery work before the Revolution.

**1758** Philadelphia Quakers stop buying and selling slaves and press for outright abolition of slavery. Quakers in other states and in London follow suit.

**1770** Anthony Benezet, a Quaker schoolteacher, begins a school for free blacks in Philadelphia and helps hundreds of black people—some free and others enslaved—learn to read and write.

**1773–1779** New England slaves petition colonial legislatures for freedom.

**1775** After the American Revolution begins in April, Lord Dunmore, the royal governor of Virginia, offers freedom to any enslaved people or indentured servants who escape and join the king's forces. Black patriots fight in all of the early battles of the Revolution. Other escaped slaves join the British army. General Washington initially refuses to allow blacks to serve but later reverses that policy. Black soldiers eventually account for between 10 and 20 percent of the Continental Army and Navy.

**1776** The Continental Congress adopts the Declaration of Independence in Philadelphia. During the debates, Congress removes a passage in Thomas Jefferson's draft that condemns the slave trade.

## CHAPTER THREE

# "MY MULATTO MAN WILLIAM"

# THE STORY OF
# BILLY LEE

I hope it will not be conceived from these observations,
that it is my wish to hold the unhappy people . . . in slavery.
I can only say that there is not a man living who
wishes more sincerely than I do, to see a plan adopted
for the abolition of it.
—George Washington in a letter to Robert Morris,
April 12, 1786

The parade was over. Sitting tall astride Nelson, his favorite chestnut horse, General George Washington had watched thousands of dejected British soldiers slowly trudge by. Humiliated, sick, hungry—some of them drunk—the once-proud British redcoats kept their eyes down. They had to pass two lines of French and American soldiers nearly a mile long and then back again. They would soon march off to prisoner-of-war camps.

*This scene by Benjamin Henry Latrobe portrays an overseer on duty near Fredericksburg, Virginia.* [Maryland Historical Society]

It was October 19, 1781, in Yorktown, Virginia. The defeated soldiers tossed their muskets onto a growing mountain of surrendered weapons, a scene that would go down as one of America's proudest moments.

Somewhere near the ranks of American soldiers and officers stood William Lee. The teenage boy purchased by Washington at auction fourteen years earlier was now a man of about thirty.

For most of those years, Billy Lee had been Washington's valet, "body servant," or personal manservant. To Washington, Billy was "my Mulatto man William." He had gone wherever George Washington went.

When Washington took command of the Continental Army in July 1775, Billy Lee had been at his master's side helping Washington dress, brush his

*The* Surrender of Lord Cornwallis *by John Trumbull hangs in the rotunda of the U.S. Capitol.*

hair, and tie it back in a ponytail. During the long war, Billy Lee usually carried the general's field glass, or telescope, and "most precious letters," perhaps those from his wife, Martha, most of which she later destroyed. Billy Lee held Washington's horse on the battlefield, and when one of Washington's mounts fell in the heat of battle at Monmouth, New Jersey, Billy Lee was there with another.

Billy Lee was in New York when Washington had the Declaration of Independence read to the troops on July 9, 1776. A constant companion, he had seen all of Washington's wartime defeats, disasters, and disappointments.

Now at Yorktown, scene of the last major battle in the American Revolution, Billy Lee was a silent witness to the final act. With the British surrender complete, George Washington had one important piece of business left. Before leaving this small Virginia tobacco port, he was going to make sure he collected twenty-year-old Lucy and eighteen-year-old Esther, along with fifteen other runaways who had left Mount Vernon.

Both young women were enslaved house servants who had fled Washington's home a few months before.

The group of runaways included Sambo Andersen.

A man like Sambo would be hard to miss. Born in Africa, Sambo Andersen had a tattooed face and wore gold earrings. Sambo was a skilled carpenter and would always claim that he was the son of an African king. He told stories of being

*Washington holds a copy of the Declaration of Independence in this French engraving circa 1785. The figure behind him holding the horse is thought to represent Billy Lee.* [Mount Vernon Ladies' Association]

captured as a boy and brought to America. His first name was derived from a common West African name that came to be widely used and only later became a slur, largely because of a series of books written in 1899 about a character named Little Black Sambo.

Esther, Lucy, and Sambo Andersen were part of a group that had willingly boarded a British warship, the *Savage*, in the spring of 1781. The captain had promised freedom to those who left Mount Vernon, Washington's plantation. Besides the seventeen refugees from Washington's home, more than twenty enslaved people from Thomas Jefferson's properties were also in Yorktown, along with thousands of others who had escaped bondage. They hoped the British would free them.

At Yorktown, these people had been put to work. Some dug trenches and built fortifications. Women did the cooking. But when supplies ran low and deadly epidemics of yellow fever, cholera, and typhus swept through the besieged town, some of the sick, starving refugees were forced out. Hundreds eventually died of disease and starvation, their bodies left rotting in the woods and fields surrounding the town.

Death and destruction were everywhere, and even in victory, Washington still had many worries. But holding the British to the surrender agreement they had signed came first. Washington insisted that "any property obviously belonging to the inhabitants of these States, in the possession of the garrison, shall be subject to be reclaimed."

That "property" meant people. At the hour of George Washington's last battle and greatest triumph—the victory that assured independence for the United States of America—thousands of enslaved people surrendered any hope of gaining their freedom.

Washington's soldiers were employed to recover many of these runaway slaves. Those from Mount Vernon and Jefferson's farms were rounded up and taken back. It would be two more years before the war officially ended, in 1783. Only then did Washington and Billy Lee, master and servant, return to Mount Vernon, arriving on Christmas Eve.

George Washington grew up in the world of Virginia plantation slavery. The son of Gus Washington, a planter, local official, and slaveholder, young George inherited ten human beings at age eleven, when his father died, along with 150 acres of property, later called Ferry Farm. Set beside Virginia's Rappahannock River, the farm was one of several owned by Gus Washington. The largest property, Little Hunting Creek, was given to Washington's older half brother Lawrence, who later renamed the estate Mount Vernon.

With little formal schooling, Washington became a surveyor

in his teens, measuring and mapping Virginia's enormous, unsettled wilderness. By age eighteen, Washington had bought more land. And by twenty-one, he had taken control of all the property and people he had inherited from his father.

Lawrence Washington died in 1752, and Washington later purchased his brother's Mount Vernon plantation for himself. Keeping up with new ideas in farming meant switching his fields to wheat from tobacco, a crop that wears out the soil. He also used large plows pulled by horses instead of relying solely on enslaved men and women working with hoes. Efficiency pleased Washington; theft did not. He noted tools that disappeared, and that the enslaved sheep shearers and spinners who were only supposed to take small amounts of "dirty wool" for themselves were keeping large amounts.

Washington was also annoyed when enslaved laborers failed to report for work. Once Washington saw a man with his arm in a sling and grabbed a rake. "Since you still have one hand free, you can guide a rake," Washington told him. "If you can use your hand to eat, why can't you use it to work?"

What Washington saw as laziness or stupidity was really resistance. Not working hard and not caring—even theft—were subtle types of rebellion, the only ways for enslaved people to fight back.

When George Washington married a rich twenty-seven-year-old widow named Martha Dandridge Custis in January

1759, he gained even more land, people, and prestige. After Martha moved to Mount Vernon with her two children, Washington was in control of more than one hundred enslaved workers.

When Washington acquired William Lee and his younger brother Frank in October 1767, he didn't note what became of Frank and Will's mother or any other siblings. Perhaps he didn't care; they were "property."

The identity of the boys' father is also unknown. It is possible that Colonel Lee was their father. This was the perverse reality that many Southern women accepted. Their fathers, husbands, or sons were the fathers of some of their servants. White children of slaveholders grew up knowing that some of their enslaved servants were their half siblings.

Another of slavery's grotesque evils was that enslaved people rarely possessed an identity of their own; they were merely viewed as an extension of the people who legally owned them. Many white people carefully recorded their family's births and deaths, often in a family Bible, in a time when there were no birth certificates or other official records for the enslaved— except receipts for when they were sold. Birth and death records were rarely kept.

[NEXT PAGES] *The main house at George Washington's Mount Vernon.*
[Author's collection]

In his autobiography, Frederick Douglass wrote, "By far the larger part of the slaves know as little of their ages as horses know of theirs, and it is the wish of most masters . . . to keep their slaves thus ignorant. I do not remember to have ever met a slave who could tell of his birthday. . . . A want of information concerning my own was a source of unhappiness to me even during childhood."

As mixed-race young men, the Lee brothers were highly desirable because they could work in the Mansion House. But we don't really know how light-skinned Frank and Billy were. Family stories described Billy as short, compact, and powerfully built without reference to his skin color. In the few portraits of Washington in which Billy appears, a horse usually obscures his body, but he is depicted with fairly dark skin. There is no way to know if the artists were trying to accurately represent an enslaved man in the background of a painting of the great man Washington.

Today, the idea that enslaved people had increased value if they looked whiter is offensive. But colonial life in Virginia, like much of America's early society, was modeled on English fashion and customs. To American slaveholders, servants in British-style livery—elaborate colorful uniforms—were considered status symbols, especially if they were lighter skinned. To a white slaveholder, appearing whiter was more physically attractive.

Thomas Jefferson expressed this attitude in his *Notes on the State of Virginia*, a series of answers to questions about American life posed by a Frenchman. "The first difference which strikes us is that of colour," wrote Jefferson in comparing whites and blacks. "And is this difference of no importance? Is it not the foundation of a greater or less share of beauty in the two races? Are not the fine mixtures of red and white ... preferable to that eternal monotony, which reigns in the countenances, that immovable veil of black which covers all the emotions of the other race?"

A large number of Mount Vernon's enslaved house workers and skilled craftsmen were of mixed race. Records show that by the time of the American Revolution, an estimated 5 percent of Virginia's enslaved population—totaling some 210,000 people in 1776—was considered mulatto. Guests at many Virginia estates were often struck by the whiteness of those serving their meals and tending the house. Louis-Philippe, a future king of France, visited Mount Vernon in 1796 and wrote, "I noticed one small boy whose hair and skin were so like ours that if I had not been told, I would never have suspected his ancestry. He is nevertheless a slave for the rest of his life."

Once at Mount Vernon, Frank and Billy Lee settled into the world of house servants. Frank was trained as a waiter and later became Mount Vernon's head butler, a crucial and prestigious job in a household like Washington's. Mount

Vernon operated with a military precision that Washington demanded. The head butler ruled the house servants and maintained the high standards Washington set for a perfectly ordered household.

As head butler, Frank was responsible for seeing that the kitchen ran smoothly, that all of the servants were doing their jobs and wearing the right clothes. The china and table linens had to be impeccably cleaned and stored away. Frank would have to make sure that there were ample supplies of wine and other drinks, as well as ice cut in the winter and stored in an icehouse for summertime use. Frank checked that the table was properly set. This meant precise placement of plates, glasses, and silver—silver that had to be spotlessly polished. He also gave the orders to the waiters. At formal meals, he would oversee the serving of many courses, ensuring that people were presented the food—soups, cheeses, fish, meat, vegetables—in the proper order and style, along with the correct type of wine for each. According to Washington's grandson, Frank was "the most polite and accomplished of all butlers."

Billy Lee had a special role as the huntsman, tending the horses and riding beside Washington on the foxhunts that Washington loved so much. Billy Lee also cared for the hunting dogs—feeding, grooming, and training them to track foxes and other animals.

Washington's grandson, George Washington Parke Custis, known as Wash, once described the hunting scene: "Will, the huntsman, . . . rode a horse called *Chinkling*, a surprising leaper, and made very much like its rider, low, but sturdy, and of great bone and muscle. Will had but one order, which was to keep with the hounds; and, mounted on *Chinkling*, a French horn at his back, throwing himself almost at length on the animal, with his spur in flank, this fearless horseman would rush, at full speed, through brake or tangled wood, in a style at which modern huntsmen would stand aghast."

There were few things that George Washington prized more than his horses and the hunt. Billy Lee had to be very good on a horse to stay with "the best horseman of his age, and the most graceful figure that could be seen on horseback," as Thomas Jefferson called Washington. For a hunt, Billy and Washington rose before the sun. Billy raced ahead, with the pack of dogs in hot pursuit of a fox. Billy, who was called opinionated, had strong ideas about which animals to pursue. When a black fox once escaped them, Billy decided that black foxes were "diabolical" and convinced Washington to stick to hunting only gray ones.

These hunts were more than just sport. The rides allowed Washington to inspect his properties. As he galloped across his fields, Washington cast a sharp eye on the lands and businesses he owned—as well as the enslaved people working those lands.

As house servants, Frank and William Lee experienced everyday life that was worlds removed from that of the enslaved field hands who worked for hours outside, rain or shine, in Virginia's hot, humid summers and freezing winters. The Lee brothers were part of a relatively small group of maids, cooks, and seamstresses who tended the main house and saw to the family's every personal need. Living near them were other enslaved people with special skills, such as masons and carpenters like Sambo Andersen. Sambo had learned his trade from a Scottish convict turned indentured servant. Training enslaved people like Sambo Andersen to do skilled labor saved the penny-wise Washington from having to hire costly outside tradesmen.

Being in the Mansion House held advantages for the Lees. It meant they would have eaten much better food and lived in much greater comfort than the field workers. And they would have worn the fancy livery, like the servants of the English nobility.

Most field hands wore threadbare rags. Typically once a year, a male farmworker received a single set of clothing that included a jacket, breeches (short pants), two shirts, a pair of stockings, and a pair of shoes. A woolen jacket was provided in winter. Women received a petticoat (an undergarment worn beneath a dress or skirt), two shifts (a type of loose-fitting dress), a jacket, one pair of stockings, and one pair of shoes.

These clothes were made from what was called "Negro cloth," the cheapest grade of cotton or linen. Still, they were expected to last over a year's hard labor. Once a year, Washington also issued each enslaved worker a new blanket that often had to serve double duty for farm chores—like gathering wood or vegetables—as well as keeping warm.

Today, most people think of an eight-hour workday as normal. But in the slaveholding world, enslaved people worked from "can see to can't see." They were expected in the fields as soon as there was light—which meant rising in the darkness and walking to work before the sun was up. And they were kept at it, under the eye of the ever-present overseers, without rest except to eat, until dark. Then they could return home.

In the summer months, when the days were longer and there was more to be done, field hands worked fifteen to sixteen hours, six days a week. Work continued in the winter, when land was cleared for the next planting season, ice was harvested from the Potomac River, and trees were cut for firewood and fencing.

Mount Vernon grew over the years to more than 8,000 acres, divided into five separate farms. Most of Washington's people lived on outlying farms. By dividing the property, Washington was looking for more efficiency, cutting the time the laborers needed to get to and from the fields they worked. Most lived in single-room, rough wooden cabins with dirt floors, far from the main house and well out of view.

A visitor from Poland described seeing these cabins around 1797. "We entered one of the huts of the Blacks, for one can not call them by the name of houses. They are more miserable than the most miserable of the cottages of our [Polish] peasants," he recorded. "The husband and wife sleep on a mean pallet [straw-filled mattress], the children on the ground; a very bad fireplace, some utensils for cooking, but in the middle of this poverty some cups and a teapot. . . . A very small garden planted with vegetables was close by, with 5 or 6 hens, each one leading ten to fifteen chickens. It is the only comfort that is permitted them, for they do not keep either ducks, geese, or pigs."

Washington and his family were well fed, dining on fine food prepared by a group of cooks. Fresh produce, pork, lamb, chicken, and fish were on the menu. Wild game was plentiful on the plantation, and one of the few ways that enslaved people could earn any money was to hunt or trap birds to sell to Washington.

Among the many cooks, an enslaved man named Hercules became Mount Vernon's head chef. A ferryman purchased from a neighbor in 1767, he was listed as the chief cook by

*A modern re-creation of a typical enslaved family's cabin at Mount Vernon.*
[Author's collection]

1787 in plantation records. Hercules had learned his skills in Mount Vernon's kitchen, and Wash Custis later described Hercules as "a celebrated artiste . . . as highly accomplished a proficient in the culinary art as could be found in the United States." He later traveled with Washington to Philadelphia to be the chief cook in the president's house.

While the food on Washington's table was abundant and finely prepared, the usual diet of the enslaved field hands consisted of a basic ration of cornmeal, salt pork, and dried fish.

On Sundays, their one regular day off, Washington's enslaved people—with a requisite pass, or "remit"—could travel to the nearby town of Alexandria and its farm markets, where they could sell chickens, eggs, and garden produce. Raising small amounts of cash gave the enslaved people a chance to supplement their meager food and clothing allowances. That may explain why some were willing to sell their teeth to their master for implanting in his own mouth.

The remit was another harsh fact of life. Woe to the black man or woman who walked the countryside without one. In Virginia and other slaveholding areas, there were no police. But there were roving slave patrollers, who made a living capturing runaways for bounties. Enslaved people called them "pattyrollers." To the pattyroller, any black person found wandering the countryside was assumed to be a runaway.

Pattyrollers had the freedom to use the lash or worse on any black person who didn't carry a pass.

"Pattyrollers is a gang of white men getting together going through the country catching slaves, and whipping and beating them up if they had no remit," recalled Charles Crawley, born enslaved in Petersburg, Virginia. In an interview recorded long after he was emancipated, he remembered, "If slaves rebelled, I done seed them whip them with a strop called 'cat-nine-tails.' Honey, this strop was about broad as your hand from thumb to little finger, and it was cut in strips up. You done seen these whips that they whip horses with? Well, they was used, too."

Billy Lee had more opportunity than most to escape. Entrusted with delivering notes and letters for Washington, he was allowed to be out on a horse alone. Well known as Washington's personal servant, he probably had less to fear from the pattyrollers.

Despite the opportunities, he and Frank never tried to run away. Others did. Escapes were a part of life at Mount Vernon and other plantations. Often younger enslaved men tried to run away, or sometimes simply leave the plantation without permission—perhaps to visit a girlfriend at a nearby plantation. Leaving for a secret visit and returning undetected might have been a thrill and a pleasure. Trying to escape completely was a different matter. The price of running and recapture was high. Even a few lashes raised welts, cut flesh, and left scars.

In 1761, Washington took out a newspaper advertisement posting a reward for the return of four men who had escaped. Washington's notice contained detailed descriptions of the men. "The two last of these Negroes were bought from an African Ship in August 1759 and talk very broken and unintelligible English; the second one, *Jack*, is Countryman to those, and speaks pretty good English, having been several Years in the Country. The other, *Peros*, speaks much better than either, indeed has little of his Country Dialect left, and is esteemed a sensible judicious Negro. . . . Whoever apprehends the said Negroes, so that the Subscriber may readily get them, shall have, if taken up in this County, Forty Shillings Reward, beside what the Law allows: and if at any greater Distance, or out of the Colony, a proportional Recompence, paid them."

The reward notice signed by Washington noted that two of the men had facial scarring and filed teeth—clear marks of African birth. All four were recaptured and returned to Mount Vernon.

Washington knew these men. One of them, Cupid, had been sick a year earlier, and Washington ordered that he be cared for properly and seen by a doctor in the main house. Was this Washington's concern for a human being? Or was he merely protecting his investment?

As a soldier, Washington had established a reputation for strict discipline among his troops. Whipping was typical for any breach of army rules, and desertion could bring a death sentence. On one occasion, Washington built a high gallows as a threat to any possible deserters in his command.

The same rigid discipline held force on the plantation. An enslaved worker who didn't share in Washington's work ethic ran the risk of the overseer's wrath—or his lash. While Washington is not known to have personally whipped or otherwise physically punished enslaved people, he did not hesitate to order his overseers to do so. "Let Abram get his deserts when taken by way of example," Washington wrote when a slave ran away in 1793. "But do not trust to Crow [an overseer] to give it him; for I have reason to believe he is swayed more by passion than by judgment in all his corrections." The same overseer, Crow, had seriously injured other slaves in flogging them.

Worse than a beating was the threat of being sold. The greatest fear was being sent to a plantation in the Deep South or West Indies. That meant almost no hope of return to family and friends. Ten years before the Revolution, Washington had ordered some of the most disobedient or "willful" enslaved people to be sold to the West Indies to work in the sugar fields, a near-certain death sentence because the work there was harder and the conditions were harsher and more deadly.

In July 1766, Washington wrote to a ship's captain sailing for the Caribbean island of Saint Kitts, explaining that he wanted one of his enslaved men to be sold. The cold calculus of slavery shows up in a grocery list of items he wanted in exchange for a human being. "With this Letter comes a Negro (Tom) which I beg the favour of you to sell, in any of the Islands you may go to, for whatever he will fetch."

Washington then itemized what he wanted in return: molasses, rum and other spirits, limes, tamarinds (a kind of fruit), and sweetmeats—nuts or fruit coated in sugar.

Washington added, "That this Fellow is both a Rogue & Runaway ... I shall not pretend to deny—But that he is exceedingly healthy, strong, and good at the Hoe, the whole neighbourhood can testifie."

A man's life was reduced to a shopping list of molasses, rum, fruits, and candy.

Later in life, Washington made a well-publicized decision not to break up enslaved families. But before the Revolution, he once organized a lottery—a raffle—to sell off some enslaved people. They had been the property of a neighbor who owed Washington money. In April 1769, Washington offered an opportunity to buy chances to win "prizes." These prizes were fifty-five people who had been divided into thirty-nine groups or lots. Some were children who were raffled off away from their parents. The list of prizes included "a Negro Girl named

*Sukey*, about 12 years old, and another named *Betty*, about 7 years old, Children of *Robin* and *Bella*."

George Washington had a carefully ordered universe, dictated by the clock, the planting seasons, and the strict bounds of slavery. But this world was about to be turned upside down.

In August 1774, the forty-two-year-old Washington went to Philadelphia to represent Virginia at the First Continental Congress. This meeting had been called to discuss united action by the thirteen colonies against the king and Parliament. Americans like Washington were growing more upset over the injustice of taxes and other "Intolerable Acts." These included the Boston Port Act, which shut down the city's port after the 1773 Boston Tea Party, and the Quartering Act, which required Americans to allow British soldiers to take over their buildings.

A war for independence was far from Washington's mind in the summer of 1774. But he was becoming angrier over how Americans were being treated by the British. He wrote to a friend that England was trying to "fix the Shackles of Slavry upon us."

Billy Lee did not have to wear shackles, but he went to Philadelphia with Washington, following his master to the meeting that set America on the course to independence. At that first Congress, Washington joined the call for a boycott of

*Washington's headquarters in Cambridge, Massachusetts.*
*Now known as Longfellow House, it is a national historic site.*

British goods. Then he and Billy returned to Mount Vernon, intent on going back to Pennsylvania for the Second Continental Congress the following May.

By then, the first shots had been fired at Lexington and Concord on April 19, 1775. War was in the air. Again, Washington wrote to his friend in England, "Unhappy it is . . . that the once happy and peaceful plains of America are either to be drenched with Blood, or Inhabited by Slaves."

Up to that time, Washington's own military experience had been limited and largely disastrous. During the French and Indian War, he had botched one mission, witnessed a bloody massacre of British troops, and then been sidelined as the conflict moved away from Virginia. But he had still acquired a hero's reputation for bravery and staunch leadership under fire. Admired, respected, and more experienced than many others, Washington was chosen to lead the Continental Army. On June 16, 1775, he accepted the job.

When Washington arrived in Cambridge, Massachusetts, on July 2, 1775, Billy Lee, now in his twenties, was by his side, as he had been for more than seven years. Like other soldiers, Billy Lee left behind a family at Mount Vernon when he went off to war. His family included a wife and child, but there is only one known reference to them. In a December 30, 1775, letter, George Washington's cousin Lund Washington—who was managing Mount Vernon—wrote to the general, "If it will give

Will any pleasure he may be told his wife and child are both very well." Billy's wife and child are never mentioned again. Even their names are lost to history.

Billy Lee tended to Washington's daily needs in a headquarters that had been the home of the president of Harvard. From day one, Washington's challenge was to whip his troops into shape. Undisciplined, with no real uniforms and few experienced officers, the army of about 15,000 militiamen Washington inherited was little more than a disorganized mob.

An army cook named Israel Trask told of seeing Billy Lee with Washington during the first winter in Cambridge. One day, some newly arrived riflemen from backwoods Virginia were walking through the yards at Harvard. Dressed in rugged deerskin hunting shirts, the Virginians met up with some locals from nearby Marblehead, Massachusetts, who made fun of the Virginians and their frontier outfits. The jokes and insults soon grew into a snowball fight. In minutes, dozens of men joined the rowdy brawl, punching, biting, and gouging one another, and soon, according to Trask, "a thousand combatants were on the field."

Out of nowhere, George Washington and Billy Lee raced up on horseback. As Billy halted to remove some fencing, Washington simply leaped the rails. "With the spring of a deer," Washington jumped from his saddle and, said Trask, "threw the reins of his bridle into the hands of his servant." As Billy

The Passage of the Delaware *by Thomas Sully, painted in 1819. The
figure at left near the cannon with his back turned is believed to represent
Billy Lee.* [Museum of Fine Arts Boston]

stood holding the horse, Washington waded into the knot of
brawlers and grabbed two of them. He took the "tall, brawny,
athletic, savage-looking riflemen by the throat, keeping them
at arm's length, alternately shaking and talking to them."

There are other brief glimpses of Billy and Washington
at war. Warily watching the British in Boston, "Washington

frequently had Billy Lee remove his mahogany and brass spy-glass from its handsome leather case so he could engage in surveillance of his adversary," biographer Ron Chernow records.

Another comes in a painting of Washington by the Connecticut-born artist John Trumbull. Set in New York near West Point in 1776, it shows Billy Lee in the background, again in Washington's shadow, his head wrapped in what looks like a bright red turban. The son of Connecticut's governor, Trumbull was a talented young artist who sketched maps for Washington and joined his military staff. Is this a true likeness of Billy? Did he wear such a hat? Or was it simply the fashion of artists to depict African Americans as foreign and exotic?

A few months after the scene depicted in that painting, Washington and his army were nearly wiped out after a series of devastating losses in and around New York City. By the fall of 1776, Washington, Billy Lee, and the defeated Continental Army had barely escaped with their lives. Many Americans had been taken prisoner and held in appalling conditions in city warehouses or on British prison ships in the East River, where as many as 11,500 men perished in one of the great

*In this portrait, painted by John Trumbull around 1780, George Washington is seen standing near the Hudson River in New York, with Billy Lee behind him. Trumbull was a soldier in Washington's army. He painted this 1776 scene from memory while studying art in London. It was the first widely copied portrait of Washington in Europe.* [The Papers of George Washington, University of Virginia; Courtesy Metropolitan Museum of Art] atrocities of the war. These British victories nearly crushed the rebellion just months after independence was declared. Washington's ability as commander was being questioned, and his army was shattered by death, desertions, and defeats.

But Billy Lee was there for the triumphant moments, too. He was with Washington on Christmas night in 1776, when the Americans crossed the Delaware, depicted in a painting made in 1819. Billy is thought to be the figure in the middle ground, shown from the rear as he helps maneuver a gun, wearing a light-colored coat and orange hat or turban.

And Billy was certainly there during the long, cold, bleak winter of 1777–1778 at Valley Forge. In a letter to Congress, Washington complained of shortages of food and clothing for his soldiers and household staff. "I cannot get as much cloth as will make Cloaths for my Servants, notwithstanding one of them that attends my person and Table, is indecently, & most shamefully naked." Washington, who was never at a loss for a uniform, doesn't name the servant, but there is a good chance that he was talking about Billy Lee.

Later in the war, Billy was with Washington when he met with six Delaware Indian chieftains, trying to win their alliance against the British. Witnessing this extraordinary scene in May 1779, Martha Washington wrote to her daughter-in-law, "The General and Billy, followed by a lot of mounted savages, rode along the line. . . . The General says it was done to

*Modern re-creation of soldiers' huts at Valley Forge, Pennsylvania. Washington spent the winter in a nearby brick house, and it is presumed that Billy Lee lived there with him and other enslaved people who came with Mrs. Washington.*

[Author's collection]

keep the Indians friendly toward us. They appeared like cut-throats all."

As the war raged, one thing was increasingly clear: Washington was rethinking his convictions about slavery. As early as 1786, he had written to wealthy Philadelphian Robert Morris, "I can only say that there is not a man living who wishes more sincerely than I do, to see a plan adopted for the abolition of it."

The contradiction between the ideals he had fought for and the enslavement of people like Billy Lee was now obvious. That conflict between belief and the reality of his life had firmly come home to Washington.

It is possible that Washington was swayed by his experience with African American soldiers who had performed far beyond his expectations. After initially refusing to allow black men to enlist, Washington was desperate for fighting men. He later allowed some African American troops to serve, usually in segregated units with white officers. By the end of the war, about one in five soldiers in Washington's army was black. One particular unit made up of enslaved men who fought in exchange for emancipation was the First Rhode Island, or the Black Regiment. They had proven to be some of Washington's best combat troops and were there at Yorktown, serving in an integrated unit.

But maybe his change of heart came from something else.

*A 1781 drawing by a French artist shows American soldiers in the Yorktown campaign, including a black infantryman from the Rhode Island Regiment.*

Perhaps Washington had reexamined his views of enslaved people because Billy Lee had proven so loyal.

His special relationship with Billy Lee was on display as the war ended in 1783 and the two men returned to Mount Vernon. Billy Lee asked Washington if a woman named Margaret Thomas, whom he had met during the war, could join him in Mount Vernon. A free black cook and seamstress from Philadelphia, Margaret Thomas had worked for Washington's staff in Cambridge. Margaret, who went by Peggy, also did sewing for the servants who were part of General Washington's household, and records show her receiving pay from October 1776 until April 1779.

Letters from Washington show that he sought to locate Margaret in Philadelphia. She was found but refused to come to Virginia—perhaps fearful of being a free black woman in a slave state. "Peggy Lee," as she was later called (though it is unknown if Peggy and Billy were married—or whatever happened to Billy's first wife), is another bystander to Washington's history who disappeared into the shadows.

After the war, Washington hoped that his years of public service were over. Having endured eight years of a soldier's life in the saddle, sleeping in tents in muddy army camps, and cold winters filled with disease and death, he was ready to settle down for the quiet life of a Virginia planter.

At the age of fifty-five, the war had taken a toll on his health. A large, robust, athletic man, Washington was plagued by headaches, stomach troubles, and bouts of rheumatism—a painful condition affecting the joints such as knees and elbows. The pain was so sharp, he sometimes carried his arm in a sling. He also had a recurrence of malaria that gave him fevers lasting weeks. And, of course, he had those famously bad teeth. His bleeding gums, lost teeth, and dental pain required costly sets of dentures. To ease his pain, he may have used laudanum, an opium drug.

The war years had also taken a toll on Mount Vernon. Buildings neglected during the war had fallen into disrepair. Washington's finances were also in bad shape; the war had been tough on his businesses. He needed to rid himself of debts that had piled up during wartime. Like many slaveholders, Washington was rich in property—in land and slaves—but cash poor.

But America was not done with Washington. In 1787, he was persuaded to return once more to Philadelphia. Washington was asked by his beloved Virginia to take part in a convention charged with revising the Articles of Confederation, the first American constitution.

Washington set off for Philadelphia. His sense of duty and the thought that the country he had helped create was in danger overcame his reluctance to leave. Again, Billy Lee went with him.

The two men stayed in the lavish home of businessman and merchant Robert Morris, the man who had helped finance the American Revolution. With its walled garden, an icehouse, and a stable with room for twelve horses, Morris's home was among the grandest in what was then America's largest, most prosperous city. Billy Lee tended to Washington's daily needs in the house, as he had for nearly twenty years. Two more of Washington's "people"—a groom named Giles and a coach driver named Paris—stayed nearby in a boardinghouse.

Washington saw no contradiction in bringing three enslaved men to Philadelphia, birthplace of the Declaration of Independence. In fact, he wanted to make sure these servants looked their best, as he attracted adoring crowds wherever he went. Two days after arriving, Washington went on a shopping expedition. Billy received a black silk handkerchief.

There is no way to know what Billy Lee, Giles, and Paris might have thought as Washington and the other men debated the future of the nation—and, with it, slavery.

For months, the Framers—as these men are known since they wrote or "framed" the Constitution—debated ideas for a new national government. Like modern political leaders, the Framers were politicians with agendas. They had special interests and different ideas about how to run what eventually would be called "a more perfect Union."

One of the most troublesome questions facing them was how the states would be represented in Congress—the new legislature where America's laws would be written. States with small populations feared that large states would be too powerful and overwhelm them if votes were based on population alone.

The result was the Great Compromise, under which Congress would be divided in two: the Senate, in which every state would get two senators and two votes; and the House of Representatives, where the number of seats and votes would be based on the state's population. Larger states would get more seats in the

House. But Congress could only enact laws if both chambers agreed—part of the "checks and balances" built into the U.S. Constitution.

This trade-off led to another sharp disagreement that threatened the convention: How would America's population be counted? And equally important, who would be counted?

Under the rules written into the final version of the United States Constitution, a census is taken every ten years. Besides simply counting how many people actually live in America, that census tally also determines how many seats each state gets in Congress and how many electors each state receives in a presidential election. Those electors—today called the Electoral College—actually cast the votes for president of the United States.

The Framers again made a bargain on who was going to be counted and how: enslaved African Americans would be counted in the census, but only as *three-fifths of a person.*

This is what they decided:

> *Representatives and direct Taxes shall be apportioned among the several States which may be included within this Union, according to their respective Numbers, which shall be determined by adding to the whole Number of free Persons, including those bound to Service for a Term of Years, and excluding Indians not taxed, three fifths of all other Persons.*

# We the People

of the United States, in order to form a more perfect Union, establish Justice, insure domestic Tranquility, provide for the common defence, promote the general Welfare, and secure the Blessings of Liberty to ourselves and our Posterity, do ordain and establish this Constitution for the United States of America.

## Article. 1.

**Section. 1.** All legislative Powers herein granted shall be vested in a Congress of the United States, which shall consist of a Senate and House of Representatives.

**Section. 2.** The House of Representatives shall be composed of Members chosen every second Year by the People of the several States, and the Electors in each State shall have the Qualifications requisite for Electors of the most numerous Branch of the State Legislature.

No Person shall be a Representative who shall not have attained to the Age of twenty five Years, and been seven Years a Citizen of the United States, and who shall not, when elected, be an Inhabitant of that State in which he shall be chosen.

Representatives and direct Taxes shall be apportioned among the several States which may be included within this Union, according to their respective Numbers, which shall be determined by adding to the whole Number of free Persons, including those bound to Service for a Term of Years, and excluding Indians not taxed, three fifths of all other Persons. The actual Enumeration shall be made within three Years after the first Meeting of the Congress of the United States, and within every subsequent Term of ten Years, in such Manner as they shall by Law direct. The Number of Representatives shall not exceed one for every thirty Thousand, but each State shall have at Least one Representative; and until such enumeration shall be made, the State of New Hampshire shall be entitled to chuse three, Massachusetts eight, Rhode Island and Providence Plantations one, Connecticut five, New York six, New Jersey four, Pennsylvania eight, Delaware one, Maryland six, Virginia ten, North Carolina five, South Carolina five, and Georgia three.

When vacancies happen in the Representation from any State, the Executive Authority thereof shall issue Writs of Election to fill such Vacancies.

The House of Representatives shall chuse their Speaker and other Officers; and shall have the sole Power of Impeachment.

**Section. 3.** The Senate of the United States shall be composed of two Senators from each State, chosen by the Legislature thereof, for six Years; and each Senator shall have one Vote.

Immediately after they shall be assembled in Consequence of the first Election, they shall be divided as equally as may be into three Classes. The Seats of the Senators of the first Class shall be vacated at the Expiration of the second Year, of the second Class at the Expiration of the fourth Year, and of the third Class at the Expiration of the sixth Year, so that one third may be chosen every second Year; and if Vacancies happen by Resignation, or otherwise, during the Recess of the Legislature of any State, the Executive thereof may make temporary Appointments until the next Meeting of the Legislature, which shall then fill such Vacancies.

No Person shall be a Senator who shall not have attained to the Age of thirty Years, and been nine Years a Citizen of the United States, and who shall not, when elected, be an Inhabitant of that State for which he shall be chosen.

The Vice President of the United States shall be President of the Senate, but shall have no Vote, unless they be equally divided.

The Senate shall chuse their other Officers, and also a President pro tempore, in the Absence of the Vice President, or when he shall exercise the Office of President of the United States.

The Senate shall have the sole Power to try all Impeachments. When sitting for that Purpose, they shall be on Oath or Affirmation. When the President of the United States is tried, the Chief Justice shall preside: And no Person shall be convicted without the Concurrence of two thirds of the Members present.

Judgment in Cases of Impeachment shall not extend further than to removal from Office, and disqualification to hold and enjoy any Office of honor, Trust or Profit under the United States: but the Party convicted shall nevertheless be liable and subject to Indictment, Trial, Judgment and Punishment, according to Law.

**Section. 4.** The Times, Places and Manner of holding Elections for Senators and Representatives, shall be prescribed in each State by the Legislature thereof; but the Congress may at any time by Law make or alter such Regulations, except as to the Places of chusing Senators.

The Congress shall assemble at least once in every Year, and such Meeting shall be on the first Monday in December, unless they shall by Law appoint a different Day.

**Section. 5.** Each House shall be the Judge of the Elections, Returns and Qualifications of its own Members, and a Majority of each shall constitute a Quorum to do Business; but a smaller Number may adjourn from day to day, and may be authorized to compel the Attendance of absent Members, in such Manner, and under such Penalties as each House may provide.

Each House may determine the Rules of its Proceedings, punish its Members for disorderly Behaviour, and, with the Concurrence of two thirds, expel a Member.

Each House shall keep a Journal of its Proceedings, and from time to time publish the same, excepting such Parts as may in their Judgment require Secrecy; and the Yeas and Nays of the Members of either House on any question shall, at the Desire of one fifth of those Present, be entered on the Journal.

Neither House, during the Session of Congress, shall, without the Consent of the other, adjourn for more than three days, nor to any other Place than that in which the two Houses shall be sitting.

**Section. 6.** The Senators and Representatives shall receive a Compensation for their Services, to be ascertained by Law, and paid out of the Treasury of the United States. They shall in all Cases, except Treason, Felony and Breach of the Peace, be privileged from Arrest during their Attendance at the Session of their respective Houses, and in going to and returning from the same; and for any Speech or Debate in either House, they shall not be questioned in any other Place.

No Senator or Representative shall, during the Time for which he was elected, be appointed to any civil Office under the Authority of the United States, which shall have been created, or the Emoluments whereof shall have been encreased during such time; and no Person holding any Office under the United States, shall be a Member of either House during his Continuance in Office.

**Section. 7.** All Bills for raising Revenue shall originate in the House of Representatives; but the Senate may propose or concur with Amendments as on other Bills.

Every Bill which shall have passed the House of Representatives and the Senate, shall, before it become a Law, be presented to the President of the

That meant that states like Virginia, with many of these "other Persons"—the phrase meant slaves, not indentured servants—received more votes in the House of Representatives, and more electors in a presidential contest, than they would have if only free white people were counted.

Some delegates objected and argued that if slaves were "property," why not count all property, including horses and houses? But the delegates from the slave states threatened to walk out of the convention if they did not get this important concession. They wouldn't accept the Constitution. And without a constitution, there would be no new national government.

The men who wrote and voted on the new Constitution were not willing to sacrifice the future of the country over the question of ending slavery. At a defining moment in American history, slavery not only continued, it was granted the Constitution's official blessing.

The Constitution also included a requirement that the federal government had to assist in the return of any escaped enslaved people, or fugitives. Article IV read, "No Person held to Service or Labour in one State, under the Laws thereof, escaping into another, shall, in Consequence of any Law or Regulation therein, be discharged from such Service or Labour, but shall

*The United States Constitution. The Three-Fifths Compromise is in Article I, Section 2.* [National Archives]

be delivered up on Claim of the Party to whom such Service or Labour may be due."

Again, the Constitution never mentioned the word *slave*, referring only to a "Person held to Service or Labour." While afraid of a new national government that was too powerful, many slaveholders still demanded a government that would put its full force behind protecting slavery, with all of its horrors.

The Constitution included one more crucial agreement about slavery without using the word. Under its terms, Congress would not limit the foreign slave trade until at least 1808—twenty years after the Constitution was ratified, or accepted by the necessary number of states.

Article I, Section 9, reads, "The Migration or Importation of such Persons as any of the States now existing shall think proper to admit, shall not be prohibited by the Congress prior to the Year one thousand eight hundred and eight, but a Tax or duty may be imposed on such Importation, not exceeding ten dollars for each Person."

This agreement gave slaveholders plenty of breathing room. They would have another twenty years to add to the enslaved population with more African captives—and the Constitution still said nothing about ending slavery altogether. By any measure, the Constitution was a win-win for American slavery and the people who drew their wealth and political power from this brutal system.

Some delegates, like George Washington and Alexander Hamilton, thought that slavery itself would eventually die out as the ideals of liberty and freedom behind the Revolution took hold in America. They had some reason for optimism. By 1787, when the Constitution was being drafted, most of the Northern states had already made the foreign slave trade illegal. Some states like Pennsylvania and Massachusetts had begun to abolish slavery along with the slave trade. The reasons for the rise of abolition—the movement to end slavery—in the Northern states are complicated. The contradiction with the ideals of the American Revolution was part of it; some slaveholders freed their enslaved people afterward. Most African Americans who fought in the Revolution and won their freedom by enlisting were from Northern states. There was also religious opposition among some Christian groups, such as the Quakers. But the economy played a role, too. The slave trade had become less profitable during the Revolution as slaveholders relied more on the natural increase of their enslaved population. The shift to paid labor, which was considered more efficient, grew more quickly as the Northern states moved into manufacturing in the earliest days of the Industrial Revolution.

The most optimistic abolitionists thought that if the slave trade ended in twenty years, slavery would eventually end.

With the future of the slave trade and slavery itself unclear, only one thing was certain when the ink was dry on the new Constitution: George Washington would be the first president of the United States. Elected in early 1789, George Washington left Mount Vernon once more for New York City, the temporary capital of the United States, where he took the oath of office on April 30, 1789.

In planning his move to New York, Washington expected his longtime manservant Billy Lee to join him. By then, a series of injuries had slowed down the man who had ridden beside Washington for more than twenty years. During a surveying trip in 1785, Lee was carrying Washington's surveying chain when he slipped on some stones and fell, breaking or dislocating one of his knees. Washington had to borrow a sled in order to get him home "as he could neither Walk, stand, or ride," Washington noted in his diary.

Three years later, while on an errand in Alexandria, Billy fell once more, this time breaking his other knee. The result, described by artist Charles Willson Peale many years later, was that "he was now a cripple & in an extraordinary manner," referring to knees that were remarkably disfigured.

Billy Lee made his way to New York, his travels slowed by the severe pain in his damaged knees. Washington's secretary, Tobias Lear, was traveling to New York with Lee. Near Philadelphia on April 19, Lear wrote to Washington's friend

Clement Biddle, "Will appears to be in too bad a state to travel at present; I shall therefore leave him—and will be much obliged to you if you will send him on to New York as soon as he can bear the journey without injury, which I expect will be in two or three days."

By the last week of May, Billy was on the mend. He finally reached New York in the middle of June and tried to resume his duties. But the stairs in the house were steep, and the busy schedule of a presidential household was far more demanding than Mount Vernon. Billy was unable to make his way in this new world. He returned to Mount Vernon in the summer of 1790.

During the rest of Washington's eight years as president, Billy Lee remained at the plantation. After Washington left office and returned home in 1797, he wrote a new version of his last will and testament. Drawn up in the summer of 1799, it provided for the eventual emancipation of the enslaved people who were his "property." Arranging for his remaining debts to be paid, he left "the use, profit and benefit of my whole Estate . . . for the term of her natural life" to Martha. His will ordered the emancipation of those enslaved people who belonged to him following Mrs. Washington's death.

But one person was singled out for special treatment in Washington's will. Rarely displaying affection in his life or letters, Washington showed his gratitude to the enslaved man who had been his constant companion. Washington wrote: "To my Mulatto man William (calling himself William Lee) I give immediate freedom."

*Immediate freedom*—what could those words have meant to William Lee? There are no documents to provide an answer. No letters, diaries, or interviews with newspapers to offer any clues.

As promised, after Washington died in December 1799, Billy was freed and received a pension, paid to him every three months, and the invitation to remain at Mount Vernon, which he accepted. By then, Billy had developed a serious drinking problem. Perhaps his badly damaged knees caused him constant pain. During his last years, while he lived at Mount Vernon and worked as a shoemaker, he gloried in telling tales of life with Washington during the war. Many guests who made the pilgrimage to Mount Vernon included veterans who were glad to pay Billy to hear his war stories.

Sadly, despite his fame, there is no accurate record of Billy Lee's death.

According to one account, Billy Lee died late in the winter of 1810. But it is more likely that Billy lived until 1828. West Ford, formerly enslaved by one of George Washington's brothers, once reported that he took care of Billy in his old age. He told of trying to ease Billy's pain by "bleeding" him. At the time, it was believed that illness or pain could be relieved if you let out a small quantity of a person's blood. One morning in the year 1828, Ford said he went out to "bleed" Billy and found him dead.

Unlike George Washington, who was first buried in a family gravesite and later laid to rest in an elaborate tomb at Mount Vernon, William Lee was buried in an unmarked grave along with other African Americans, most of them enslaved people whose remains were placed in a separate burial ground at Mount Vernon.

*George Washington's tomb at Mount Vernon.* [Author's collection]

Even experts at the plantation are unclear about Billy's remains.

This uncertainty—the wide disparity in these dates 1810 and 1828 and the location of Billy Lee's remains—shows again how enslaved people lived in the shadows of the white world. Perhaps the most famous enslaved man in America at the time, William Lee was not granted the most basic recognition of his birth or death.

*The Slave Memorial at Mount Vernon. The slave cemetery, where the remains of Billy Lee and other enslaved people are probably buried, is behind the picket fence at the rear of the memorial.*
[Author's collection]

IN MEMORY OF
THE AFRO-AMERICANS
WHO SERVED AS SLAVES
AT MOUNT VERNON
THIS MONUMENT MARKING THEIR
BURIAL GROUND
DEDICATED
SEPTEMBER 21 1983
MOUNT VERNON
LADIES' ASSOCIATION

# SLAVERY IN AMERICA TIME LINE
## 1777–1800

**1777**  The constitution of Vermont outlaws slavery. Vermont becomes the fourteenth state in 1791.

**1779**  John Laurens, a young officer in Washington's military circle, proposes emancipating and arming 3,000 African Americans to fight the British in South Carolina; the proposal is rejected by South Carolina's legislature.

**1780**  Pennsylvania adopts a gradual emancipation law.

**1783**  The American Revolution officially ends. Massachusetts abolishes slavery.

**1784**  Connecticut and Rhode Island enact gradual emancipation laws. The Pennsylvania Abolition Society is formed; Benjamin Franklin and Dr. Benjamin Rush, another signer of the Declaration of Independence, are key organizers.

**1787**  Meeting in Philadelphia, the Constitutional Convention agrees to three major points that concern slavery, although the word is never used in the Constitution:
- The census will count three-fifths of a state's enslaved population in calculating how many seats each state gets in the House of Representatives.
- Congress cannot end the slave trade for twenty years.
- Runaways or fugitives who cross state lines must be surrendered to their owners if caught.

In a separate act, the Continental Congress enacts the Northwest Ordinance, which outlaws slavery in the territories north of the Ohio and east of the Mississippi Rivers.

**1789**  George Washington is sworn in as the first president on April 30 in New York City.

**1790**  Philadelphia becomes the temporary capital of the United States.

**1791**
- The Haitian Revolution begins. After years of violent fighting, former slaves and free people of color defeat French, Spanish, and British armies and declare the second independent republic in the Americas.
- The Bill of Rights, the first ten amendments to the Constitution, is ratified, or approved, by the states in December.

**1792**  Kentucky becomes the fifteenth state in June, with slavery allowed.

**1793**  The Fugitive Slave Act is passed. Under this law, the federal government must help recapture fugitives; to hide or "harbor" a fugitive is illegal.

**1794**  Eli Whitney patents his design for the cotton gin. This machine increases the demand for enslaved labor to plant and harvest cotton.

**1796**
- Tennessee becomes the sixteenth state, with slavery allowed.
- John Adams of Massachusetts is elected the second American president. Thomas Jefferson becomes vice president.

**1799**  New York adopts a law for gradual emancipation.

**1800**
- In January in Philadelphia, a group of free blacks presents Congress with a petition condemning slavery, the slave trade, and the Fugitive Slave Act. The petition dies in committee.
- In June, the new city of Washington, D.C., becomes the official capital of the United States. President Adams moves into what will later be called the White House in November.
- In August, a large armed rebellion in Virginia led by an enslaved blacksmith named Gabriel is put down. Gabriel and many of his followers are executed.
- The presidential election of 1800 ends in a controversial tie between Thomas Jefferson and Aaron Burr, who are in the same party.
- The census shows a population of 5.3 million Americans, including a little more than 1 million blacks, about 19 percent of the total U.S. population; some 90 percent of them are enslaved. Virginia is the most populous state with 880,000 residents, nearly 347,000 of them enslaved.

# CHAPTER FOUR

# "ABSCONDED FROM THE HOUSEHOLD OF THE PRESIDENT"

# THE STORY OF ONA JUDGE

Ten dollars will be paid to any person who
will bring her home.

—PRESIDENT GEORGE WASHINGTON'S ADVERTISEMENT
FOR THE RETURN OF AN ENSLAVED
WOMAN WHO ESCAPED IN PHILADELPHIA,
*THE PENNSYLVANIA GAZETTE*, MAY 23, 1796

I wanted to be free . . . wanted to learn to read and write.
—ONA JUDGE STAINES

It was dinnertime on a pleasant Philadelphia evening in May 1796. A young woman left the house where she worked as a maid and seamstress. Neatly attired, she wore the proper clothing of a house servant in the grand home of one of the city's finest families.

*This idealized painting shows Washington among enslaved workers in the field.*
[Library of Congress, Prints & Photographs Division, LC-DIG-pga-02419]

89

In her twenties, with dark hair, light skin, and freckles, she was a mulatto, the daughter of a black woman from Virginia and a white Englishman. She walked quickly, alone but unafraid. The sight of a young mixed-race or black woman by herself on the streets of Philadelphia in 1796 was not unusual.

Philadelphia was a prosperous place of broad, paved streets, well-tended homes, and large brick buildings. As she walked, the young lady's maid passed the site where the Declaration of Independence had been written and adopted twenty years earlier. She was about the same age as the United States of America.

America's largest city, Philadelphia had gained greater prestige with the Constitutional Convention in 1787. And three years later, it became the young republic's capital, seat of the Congress and the presidential mansion and offices. Walking down Philadelphia's streets, one might see such great men as Jefferson, Madison, and, of course, President George Washington as they went about the nation's business.

But Philadelphia's prosperity and prominence were not why this young African American woman could walk freely down its streets. In 1780, Pennsylvania had made slavery illegal, the first state to do so. The state and its largest city were the center of Quaker influence and power in America. Although relatively few in number in America, the Quakers, or the Society of Friends, had been leaders in America's early antislavery movement.

*The building on the right in this 1848 lithograph is Congress Hall, originally designed as a courthouse, which Congress occupied in 1790.*

[Library of Congress, Prints & Photographs Division, 2013651654]

Free people of color were a common sight on the streets of the City of Brotherly Love. There was no fear of the pattyrollers checking every black person to see if he or she had the required remit, or pass, to be out alone. Philadelphia was certainly a place where a young African American woman could go about her business without attracting much notice. In fact, this woman had gone to a nearby theater sometimes, given tickets by the lady of the house where she served.

As she made her way across the city, the woman kept her eyes and head down. She spoke to no one until she reached the address she had been given. The friends who had pointed out the house to her may have been the same people who had earlier carried her bags away from the home where she worked. And it was those same friends—perhaps members of Philadelphia's growing circle of free blacks—who helped the young woman book passage on the *Nancy,* a small ship that would soon sail north for New England.

Under the cover of night, the young woman boarded the ship and was given a place belowdecks by a friendly captain named John Bowles. While Captain Bowles was white, some of the *Nancy*'s crew members may have been free men of color. African Americans had manned ships in the American Revolution, and these "Black Jacks" now worked the merchant ships that crowded Philadelphia's busy port.

Before dawn on a morning sometime in early June 1796, the

ship sailed for Portsmouth, New Hampshire, a vibrant New England port city a few days' voyage away. Captain Bowles had built a profitable trade carrying freight back and forth between Portsmouth and the nation's capital. After unloading his cargo of leather products like saddles and bridles, Captain Bowles would return to Philadelphia in a few weeks, then make his regular run back to Portsmouth in July.

But as he set the familiar course for Portsmouth, the master of the *Nancy* had broken the law. Along with its cargo of merchandise, the *Nancy* carried a fugitive passenger, an enslaved woman escaping her bondage. To assist a slave in running away was a federal crime.

And the *Nancy*'s passenger was no ordinary runaway. She was Ona Judge. Visitors to the president's mansion in Philadelphia, where George Washington and his wife, Martha, lived, would have instantly recognized her as Mrs. Washington's maid.

Most likely, Ona Judge would be the first person Martha Washington saw in the morning and the last she saw at night. As her personal maid, Ona Judge—her given name was Oney but she preferred Ona—was expected to be up early to help dress her mistress. Afterward, Mrs. Washington spent an hour at her devotions, reading the Bible and the Book of Common Prayer used in the Episcopal Church.

The presidential household in Philadelphia worked on a

*An engraved portrait of Martha Washington from a painting by Gilbert Stuart.*
[Library of Congress, Prints & Photographs Division, LC-USZ62-113386]

strict schedule—just like Washington's Virginia home. George Washington tolerated no lateness or laziness from his cabinet officers, secretaries, or enslaved servants. His wife's standards were no different. So it wasn't long before Ona Judge's disappearance on that May evening was noticed.

When Martha Washington—or "Lady Washington" as she was known to most people—realized what had happened, she was more than simply annoyed. She was shocked and felt betrayed. Why would a young woman who was treated with genuine decency—even affection, in Mrs. Washington's view—want to leave an honored position in this great home?

Martha Washington had known Ona since the young woman was born at Mount Vernon. To her eyes, Ona lived a fairly comfortable life in the Washington household. Her duties were light. She was treated generously. Lady Washington had given theater tickets to Ona and some of the other enslaved servants. As Martha Washington once wrote, her enslaved people should have "gratitude for the kindness that may be shewed [showed] to them."

President Washington was also put out. Soon after Ona's escape was discovered, he wrote, "The ingratitude of the girl, who was brought up & treated more like a child than a Servant."

For a man who had fought so long and hard for freedom, it is astonishing Washington could not comprehend that an enslaved person might want the same right. And worse—he was not going to simply accept that one of his slaves, a young woman he saw as little more than a child, would challenge his authority.

The president took action. On May 23, 1796, Washington's steward placed a notice in a Philadelphia newspaper offering a ten-dollar reward (about 180 dollars in today's money) for the return of the runaway known as Oney Judge. The prominent

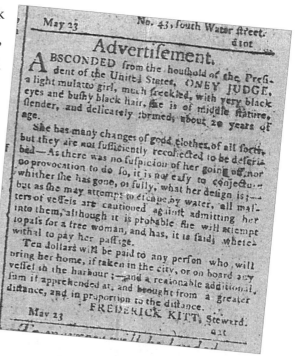

advertisement began with the words "Absconded from the household of the President."

The advertisement hinted at Washington's annoyance and surprise. "There was no suspicion of her going off, nor no provocation to do so," the ad said. The president also guessed, correctly, that Ona might book passage on a ship and had the funds—the "wherewithal"—to do so.

George and Martha Washington had every legal right to expect the speedy return of Ona Judge. Three years earlier, President Washington had signed into law the Fugitive Slave Act of 1793. It allowed him—and all slaveholders—to recover their property with the full use of the federal courts. This law made it a federal offense for anyone to assist a runaway.

*The Fugitive Slave Act of 1793*
SEC. 4. And be it further enacted, *That any person who shall knowingly and willingly obstruct or hinder such claimant, his agent, or attorney, in so seizing or arresting such fugitive from labor, or shall rescue such fugitive from such claimant, his agent or attorney, when so arrested pursuant to the authority herein given and declared; or shall harbor or conceal such person after notice that he or she was a fugitive from labor, as aforesaid, shall, for either of the said offences, forfeit and pay the sum of five hundred dollars. Which penalty may be recovered by and for the benefit of such claimant, by*

*action of debt, in any Court proper to try the same, saving*
*moreover to the person claiming such labor or service his right*
*of action for or on account of the said injuries, or either of them.*
 *Approved [signed into law by President George Washington],*
*February 12, 1793.*

What Martha Washington said or wrote directly about Ona's escape is not documented. However, President Washington made clear in several letters that his wife was extremely disturbed and had a theory about what happened to Ona. Martha Washington told her husband that a "Frenchman" was at fault. With no real evidence, she believed a man—a "Seducer"—must have been behind Ona's secret departure. Perhaps Ona was even pregnant with this mysterious Frenchman's child. Washington wrote to a government official whose help he sought, "There is no doubt in this family of her having been seduced and enticed off by a Frenchman."

In the eyes of George and Martha Washington, that was the only reason why Ona Judge would leave their "family." Why would the trusted seamstress and maidservant of Martha Washington, who had been at her side for more than ten years, run away in the first place?

Ona Judge was a Custis "dower slave," meaning that she was part of the estate belonging to Martha's first husband. When Daniel Custis died, he left Ona to Martha. As long as Martha was alive, Ona remained her property. After Martha's death, a dower slave would be part of the Custis estate once more and passed on to the rightful heir.

Ona was born Oney Judge at Mount Vernon around 1773 or 1774—the exact date of her birth, like that of many enslaved people, was never recorded. Her mother, Betty, was a seamstress. Her father was a white indentured servant, a tailor named Andrew Judge, who had come to America from Leeds, England, in 1772 and gained his freedom after fulfilling the terms of his four-year contract at Mount Vernon. Before leaving, Andrew Judge secured a place in history as the man who sewed George Washington's buff-and-blue Virginia militia uniform, when the future general went off to the Continental Congress in 1775. Washington wore the uniform during his time in Philadelphia, and it had the intended effect, as John Adams wrote to his wife, Abigail. "Col. Washington appears at Congress in his Uniform and, by his great Experience and Abilities in military Matters, is of much service to Us." Andrew Judge left the plantation to start a farm of his own soon after Ona was born. He left mother and child behind but was probably permitted to visit on occasion.

As a seamstress, Betty spent much of her time spinning thread, weaving cloth, and tailoring clothes for the Washington family. Martha Washington wore the elegant fashions of the day, including gowns made of silk and other luxury fabrics. One of her dresses, still intact at Mount Vernon, was made of lustrous brown silk with lace trim. Working with these fabrics and caring for them properly required great skill. According to one biography of Martha Washington, "Pieces of fabric cut from her dresses and passed down through the family as mementos are a beautiful assortment of lampas and damask silks—white with red and pink roses, pale ivory with narrow ivory stripes and delicate bouquets."

As a dower slave from the Custis estate, Betty had come to Mount Vernon after George and Martha married in 1759, moving there with her mistress. Even though Ona's father had obtained his freedom around the time she was born, Ona was considered property of the slaveholder under Virginia law. Since her mother was a Custis dower slave, so was Ona. Betty and Andrew Judge had a second child, a girl named Philadelphia, or Delphy, six years younger than Ona and also a dower slave. Ona also had an older half brother named Austin, but his father's identity is unknown.

As a child, Ona's days were spent near her mother, gradually learning simple household tasks like churning butter, making soap and candles, washing laundry, and preparing food. Eventually she learned spinning thread and weaving cloth, and like her mother, Ona became a talented seamstress. George Washington once described her as being a "perfect Mistress of her needle."

After Washington was elected president, he moved to New York, the nation's temporary capital, arriving in April 1789. Martha made the trip a month later, bringing along her two grandchildren, Nelly and Wash Custis. Nelly and Wash were the orphaned children of Martha's son Jacky Custis, who died of illness at Yorktown in 1781. The two of them were raised by George and Martha as their own. Also with Martha came seven enslaved people, including Ona and Austin. Ona's mother and her younger sister remained behind at Mount Vernon.

By this time a teenager, Ona had moved from performing household duties to becoming Lady Washington's personal attendant. Like all of the enslaved people who settled into the rented presidential household on Cherry Street near the East River, Ona would have shared rooms on the third floor.

In February 1790, the entire household moved to a larger, more fashionable mansion on Broadway near Wall Street. Previously the home of the French ambassador, it was here the president and his wife would regularly entertain. The stream of prominent guests included foreign dignitaries and members of the new government, such as New Yorker Alexander Hamilton, the secretary of the treasury; and fellow Virginians Thomas Jefferson, Washington's secretary of state; and James

*The Alexander Macomb House, located on Broadway in New York City,
served as the second presidential mansion, from February to August 1790.
This engraving was made in 1831, when the mansion became a hotel.*

Madison, then a member of Congress and one of Washington's closest political advisers. Mrs. Washington's regular visitors included Abigail Adams, wife of John Adams, the first vice president, who quickly became a close friend.

Whether at formal dinners, followed by coffee served to the ladies, or at afternoon teas, Ona Judge would have silently tended the guests, mingling among some of the most powerful men in America and their wives.

By then, Christopher Sheels had replaced Billy Lee as Washington's regular valet. Related to Billy by marriage, the fourteen-year-old Christopher had been born into the third generation of Mount Vernon's enslaved people. His mother, Alice, had been a spinner, and his father is thought to have been a white wagon driver working at Mount Vernon. His grandmother, a cook known as Old Doll, was a Custis servant who had come to Mount Vernon with Martha.

Christopher had traveled to New York as a valet in training. He was being groomed to take Billy Lee's place when Billy's knees gave out, and there was an inevitable changing of the guard.

The pace of life in New York was far busier than the slower tempo of Mount Vernon. Back at the Virginia plantation, there were rides, hunts, meals, and parties, but life was rarely hectic. As president, Washington had a full schedule of regular engagements with people at every level of the brand-new

American government. Just as a president and First Lady host state balls and entertain regularly today, George and Martha Washington had to attend to the business of government and maintain a busy social schedule. An invitation to the Washingtons' home for an afternoon tea or a formal dinner was an extraordinary honor.

For Ona Judge, life at the center of the nation's new capital was entirely different from the plantation world of Mount Vernon. But her duties were the same. As lady's maid to the president's wife, her tasks included caring for the expensive silk and woolen clothing and the linens worn closest to the body, as well as delicate lace and handkerchiefs. Plumper as she got older, Mrs. Washington also wore a corset—an undergarment to cinch in a woman's waist—and Ona would be the one who laced it tight.

Not only did she tend to Martha's clothing, but Ona was responsible for Martha Washington's makeup—powders and rouge were popular at the time. Although Ona had always done Mrs. Washington's hair, Martha Washington began to employ a hairdresser in New York. And at the end of the day, Ona would help Martha Washington undress and get into her nightgown before assisting her into bed.

[NEXT PAGES] *This painting,* The Republic Court (Lady Washington's Reception Day), *by Daniel Huntington (circa 1861), depicts life in New York when Washington was president.* [The Brooklyn Museum]

Ona was also expected to travel with the First Lady, although that term was not yet used for the president's wife. She accompanied Martha Washington on daily errands in New York, a rapidly growing city that was bustling with shops importing the latest in European fashions and fabrics. It was a far cry from Mount Vernon, where the nearest town was Alexandria, still a fairly small village with few luxuries.

Even more important were the social calls, teas, and luncheons. While the wives of diplomats, legislators, and members of Washington's cabinet visited or entertained Martha Washington, Ona would meet with their servants, some of them free black people. Ona Judge, the teenage lady's maid of America's most famous woman, was getting her first taste of freedom. And she wanted more.

In August 1790, the seat of American government shifted from New York to Philadelphia, which was America's most sophisticated city at the time. Packing up the household again, George and Martha Washington moved into the new President's House with the entire group of enslaved people to tend them. Once occupied by British generals when they controlled Philadelphia during the Revolution, it was the same large mansion on High Street (later called Market Street) that Washington and Billy Lee had stayed in during the Constitutional Convention in 1787.

Dismantled long ago, the President's House is marked today

by an exhibit that shows the foundation of the building and is adjacent to the museum housing Philadelphia's Liberty Bell. When the Washingtons lived in the three-story brick house, it was one of Philadelphia's grandest residences, surrounded by brick walls. Rented from wealthy financier and merchant Robert Morris—who obligingly moved to another house on the same block to make way for the Washingtons—it would serve as both the president's office and the official residence. Two large public rooms on the first two floors had been enlarged with fashionable bow windows overlooking a garden. The family resided on the second floor with bedrooms, dressing rooms, and drawing rooms. One for Martha featured a new cast-iron stove to heat the sometimes cold and drafty house. The servants—free and enslaved—lived in outbuildings, including space over the adjacent stables, where Washington's carriages and horses were kept.

The Washingtons lived in the mansion with Nelly and Wash and a household staff that included several enslaved people— Ona; another maid, Molly; the head chef, Hercules; his son, Richmond; Washington's valet, Christopher Sheels; Ona's half brother, Austin; and Paris, a coachman.

But the presence of slaves in Philadelphia would create a problem for Washington. There was a ten-year-old law in Pennsylvania that said slaves brought into the state would be

*Washington stayed in the Philadelphia residence of Robert Morris during the Constitutional Convention, and it became the President's House when Washington returned in 1790. The house, shown here in an 1830 drawing, was later torn down.*

free after living there for six months. This created a public relations embarrassment of sorts—and a legal hurdle.

Washington had to find a way around it. How else could he retain his "family"? He feared that some of the servants he had brought to Philadelphia might leave if given the opportunity. Washington did not think his slaves "would be benefitted by the change," he wrote to his personal secretary. "Yet the idea of freedom might be too great a temptation for them to resist."

*The Pennsylvania Act for the Gradual Abolition of Slavery, March 1, 1780.*
[The President's House, Philadelphia]

While we like to think of Washington as the champion of liberty and the honest little boy of the cherry tree legend who couldn't tell a lie, the president deliberately dodged the law in Philadelphia. He did so by playing a version of hide-and-seek, issuing orders that some of the enslaved people would be moved in and out of Philadelphia to avoid detection.

"I wish to have it accomplished under pretext that may deceive both them and the Public," wrote the president. He wanted this plan known only to personal secretary Tobias Lear and Martha.

The plan Washington hatched meant sending some of the enslaved servants back to Mount Vernon every six months, or having them travel with Mrs. Washington outside of Pennsylvania. The law applied only to slaves over age twenty-eight, so Ona was exempt. Washington was most concerned about Hercules and Paris. They were Custis dower slaves, and if they escaped, he would have to repay the Custis estate. His elaborate ruse worked, even though Washington was certainly breaking the letter of the law. But who was going to challenge the most admired man in America over a handful of house servants?

Ona and the others surely knew about the law. Philadelphia was home to more than a thousand free blacks by this time. The real possibility of freedom was there for them to see every day. Free black men like James Forten, who was a sailor in the American Revolution, had prospered in business. But the thought of escaping from the Washingtons must still have seemed like an impossible dream.

For six years, the deception continued. By 1796, Washington's second term in office neared its end. America's first president was tired. He wanted only to return to Mount Vernon and the quiet life of retirement as a farmer. Thoughts of a third term were quickly dismissed—even though there was no term limit for the presidency at the time, as there is today. Plans were being made for the departure of all the enslaved people who would return to Mount Vernon. But not everyone was going back. A plan for Ona's future was unfolding, and it was around this time that Ona got wind of it.

Late in his life, Washington had pledged not to sell any more enslaved people from Mount Vernon. He also claimed he did not want to break up families on the plantation. But gifts of servants were apparently a different matter, especially if the servants were Custis dower slaves like Ona Judge. Before returning to Virginia, Martha Washington made it known that Ona would be presented as a wedding gift to her granddaughter Eliza.

It is hard to contemplate that a person like Ona Judge was seen by her mistress as an appropriate gift—no different from expensive china, a parcel of land, or a fine horse—to be passed along to a family member. What enslaved blacks felt or thought about leaving their home, friends, and family was simply not taken into account. Ona was to be given to Eliza, who had a reputation among Mount Vernon's enslaved people as ill-tempered. The thought of becoming Eliza's property did not sit well with Ona. Once she learned of her fate, she set out to escape.

Ona never revealed much about those who had helped her. But Philadelphia's black freemen had begun to help enslaved people escape. Eventually they would form the core of the famous Underground Railroad, the people who helped runaways make their way north to freedom.

Having made good her escape on the *Nancy,* Ona arrived in Portsmouth, New Hampshire, and soon found work as a seamstress. Alone, with no friends or family, she must have had incredible courage and resourcefulness. American history is filled with stories of immigrants and pioneers who took great risks to make new lives in America. But Ona Judge had taken a much greater risk. A single young woman, probably illiterate, she was escaping from the household of America's most famous and powerful man. She must have known the price of her daring. Being caught might mean at best a return to bondage, or worse, being sold deeper South or to the West Indies, if Washington decided she was too much trouble.

And the risk proved real. Not long after Ona arrived in Portsmouth, she was walking through the bustling seaport and shipbuilding center. Passing her on the street one day was

Elizabeth Langdon, the daughter of New Hampshire Senator John Langdon. Elizabeth Langdon recognized Ona. Her father was friends with President Washington, and Elizabeth had visited Martha Washington and Eliza Custis.

Accounts of this chance encounter differ. In one version, Ona ducks away from the young woman without speaking. But in another, Elizabeth Langdon asks Ona why she is in New Hampshire. Ona defiantly tells her that she has run away. "I wanted to be free, missis."

Whichever version is true, it was not long before word of Ona Judge's presence in Portsmouth reached the president. Wasting no time, Washington contacted Joseph Whipple, Portsmouth's collector of customs, to seek his help in the matter. Joseph Whipple was the brother of a signer of the Declaration of Independence, William Whipple. A wealthy merchant who had continued his family's long role in the slave trade, William Whipple later fought as a general in the Revolution. The family's prominence had led to Joseph's appointment to the lucrative post as collector of customs.

On September 1, 1796, the president asked Whipple to seize Ona and put her on board a ship bound for Philadelphia or Alexandria, Virginia, near Mount Vernon. Washington promised to reimburse the man for his efforts. Financial incentives aside, it would have been difficult for anyone to say no to America's greatest man.

Eager to please the president, Joseph Whipple located Ona in a matter of hours. Finding a fugitive black woman in the city was not difficult. New Hampshire was a largely white state, with some 360 free African Americans in Portsmouth. When Joseph Whipple met Ona, however, he was convinced of her "thirst for compleat freedom." He also believed that there was no seducer involved—and told Washington as much.

Once again proving her extraordinary will and courage, Ona bargained with Whipple. Here she was, a young runaway with few resources. But she was not going to surrender. She persuaded Whipple that she would return to Mount Vernon—but only on the condition that she would be granted her freedom.

When he got this news, George Washington was furious. Why was Whipple bargaining with a young female slave in his name?

A few months later, in November 1796, Washington wrote to Whipple, angry that he had not already secured Ona's return. The president told Whipple to take more extreme action to force her back to the plantation. But he still cautioned him. "I do not mean . . . that such violent measures should be used as would excite a mob or riot," Washington wrote to Whipple.

By then, Ona had made plans to marry John Staines, a free black man and merchant seaman. Ona and John were legally wed in January 1797, but Ona was still the property of the Custis estate in the eyes of the law. Any children she bore would also be Custis property.

While this drama unfolded in New Hampshire, other members of the Washington household were demonstrating a taste for freedom. Few people were more valuable to the First Family than Hercules, Mount Vernon's master chef.

He had also been taken to Philadelphia in 1790. In Washington's deceptive scheme, Hercules had been one of those sent back and forth to Mount Vernon from time to time. Fearful that Hercules would escape in Philadelphia, Washington had him sent back to Mount Vernon in December 1796. He had been demoted from the kitchen to a field hand so Washington's overseers could keep a better eye on him. But sometime around Washington's birthday, on February 22, 1797, Hercules made good his escape.

He vanished without a trace. Washington never pursued Hercules with quite the same intensity that he went after Ona. Hercules, unlike Ona, was not a dower slave but part of Washington's personal property. Although his escape was a loss, Washington would not have to pay the Custis estate for Hercules. But he did make some effort to track down his much-admired household cook. In running away, Hercules had not just left behind his kitchen duties with America's First Family; he had left behind a family. A visitor to Mount Vernon once asked the young daughter of Hercules, who was still enslaved,

*This painting of Hercules is by America's most famous portraitist, Gilbert Stuart, who made several famous paintings of Washington and other noted Americans of the period.* [Museo Thyssen–Bornemisza/Scala, Florence]

if she missed her father. She told him, "Oh! Sir, I am very glad, because he is free now."

And Christopher Sheels, the young man who had taken Billy Lee's favored place as valet, also made a grab for freedom. After he asked Washington for permission to marry a young woman from another plantation, Sheels and the young woman plotted to flee aboard a ship in September 1799. But a note describing their plot was dropped on the ground, and Washington found it. The escape was foiled, and Sheels remained at Mount Vernon.

Long after he left office, Washington kept working to bring Ona back. Two years after she escaped from Philadelphia, the president asked his nephew, Burwell Bassett Jr., to seize the woman. Bassett was planning a business trip to New Hampshire, and Washington told him to find her and bring her back, along with any children she may have had.

But the times were changing. And even Washington's friends and admirers had come to weigh their changing beliefs against Washington and the Fugitive Slave Act. During dinner with Senator Langdon, Bassett revealed his intentions to recapture Ona. Despite his friendship with Washington, the senator was not about to be party to the kidnapping of a woman, who by this time had a baby. Senator Langdon sent one of his servants to tell Ona Judge about the plan to capture her. She fled to the neighboring town of Greenland, where she and her baby went into hiding in the home of a free black family. She stayed there until Bassett left New Hampshire and her husband returned from sea.

George Washington's death in December 1799 ended the efforts to return Ona Judge Staines to slavery. Ona had told Whipple earlier that she would rather die than return to slavery. Many years after Washington died, Ona told a newspaper, "They never troubled me any more after he was gone."

In his will, George Washington left his enslaved people—with the notable exception of Billy Lee—to his wife, Martha, ordering that they be freed after her death. But Martha Washington did not wait to do so. In January 1801, she emancipated her late husband's servants. But it was not out of charity or a change of heart. She was afraid. She told her friend Abigail Adams in December 1800 that "she did not feel as tho her Life was safe in their Hands." Martha Washington feared that some of the enslaved servants, knowing that her death would bring their freedom, might do something to speed up the process.

One of those freed was Sambo Andersen, who decided to remain near Mount Vernon because his wife and children were still Custis dower slaves. Eventually he was able to earn enough money to purchase the freedom of some of his children and their descendants.

When Martha Washington died in May 1802, some of the Custis dower slaves were divided among her four grandchildren, and others were freed. Among them was a man named William Custis Costin, who was the mixed-race son of Martha Washington's son Jacky Custis. That made William Costin Martha's grandson. In 1800, Costin had married Delphy Judge, Ona's younger sister. Delphy was also freed in 1802 with her husband. That means Martha's mixed-race grandson married her former maid's sister. That was the world of plantation slavery.

What would have happened to Ona Judge Staines had she been returned to Mount Vernon? After her husband, Jack, died in 1803, Ona suffered through difficult times of personal loss and poverty. As an old woman, she had to rely upon the charity of her church to survive. She frequently attended religious services and became a devout Christian. She learned how to read. She had complete control over her time and could decide how to spend it, taking up hobbies like painting. She was a free woman. She could come and go as she pleased. Yet the ex-slave admitted that her life as a free woman was much more difficult than it would have been had she stayed with the Washingtons.

In 1846, an abolitionist minister named Benjamin Chase visited Ona and reported, "I have recently made a visit to one of Gen. Washington's, or rather Mrs. Washington's slaves. *It is a* woman, nearly white, very much freckled, and probably, (for she does not know her age,) more than eighty. She now resides with a colored woman by the name of Nancy Jack... and is maintained as a pauper by the county of Rockingham. She says that she was a chambermaid for Mrs. Washington; that she was a large girl at the time of the revolutionary war; that when Washington was elected President, she was taken to Philadelphia, and that, although well enough used as to work and living, she did not want to be a slave always, and she supposed if she went back to Virginia, she would never have a chance to escape."

Ona's story set alongside that of Billy Lee leaves a great puzzle: Why did Washington's faithful manservant Billy Lee choose to stay, while Ona Judge took enormous risks to escape? Why did two people in relatively similar circumstances take such different paths?

The answer is a mystery. Both Ona and Billy would have had to balance the risks and rewards of escaping bondage. We will probably never know what Billy thought about freedom. While still enslaved, he enjoyed a certain rank and privileges. He even had a measure of "respect" from the white people who controlled his life. Billy certainly had opportunities to escape if he had chosen to try. On the other hand, he enjoyed some security, comfort, and occasional moments of independence— things that most enslaved people never experienced.

While Billy was silent to history, Ona was able to answer for herself. Later in her life she said, "No, I am free, and have, I trust, been made a child of God by the means."

She died poor but free on February 25, 1848.

# SLAVERY IN AMERICA TIME LINE
## 1801–1816

**1801** After many votes in the House of Representatives, Thomas Jefferson is elected the third president.

**1803**
- Ohio becomes the seventeenth state, a free state; however, blacks are excluded from citizenship, meaning they cannot vote or serve on juries.
- The United States purchases the Louisiana Territory from France, doubling the size of the country and opening up vast new lands that will fuel the debate over the future of slavery in America.

**1804** New Jersey passes a plan for gradual emancipation.

**1807**
- The British Parliament bans the slave trade on March 25.
- On March 3, 1807, Thomas Jefferson signed into law Congress's ban on the importation of slaves, to take effect January 1, 1808.

**1808**
- On January 1, the United States ban on the foreign slave trade takes effect.
- In December, James Madison, another slaveholder from Virginia, is elected the fourth president.

**1810** The third United States census counts a national population of more than 7.2 million people. Approximately 1.4 million African Americans live in America—about 19 percent of the total population; nearly 1.2 million are enslaved.

**1811** In what is considered one of the largest rebellions of enslaved African Americans, between 300 and 500 enslaved people in Louisiana, armed with cane knives and other farm tools, attack their white owners. Inspired by Haiti's rebellion, this uprising is put down by a combination of local and federal troops. More than sixty of the rebels are killed, their heads displayed on pikes alongside roads outside New Orleans as a warning against future revolts.

**1812**
- Louisiana becomes the eighteenth state, with slavery permitted.
- War is declared against Great Britain in what becomes known as the War of 1812. During this war, an estimated 15 percent of American sailors are black men.

**1814**

During the War of 1812, British troops attack and burn Washington, D.C., and the White House. Also during the war, future president Andrew Jackson leads an attack on Seminole Indians in western Florida.

**1815**

In January, "free men of color" and enslaved blacks join Andrew Jackson's forces in the Battle of New Orleans, in which the British army suffers one of its greatest defeats. Under the terms of the treaty with England, enslaved people who had escaped to the British are returned to their owners; some who had been promised freedom by Andrew Jackson remain in slavery.

**1816**
- The Negro Fort, a small old Spanish fort in Florida that is home to hundreds of runaways, is destroyed during a battle with federal troops led by Andrew Jackson in part of a war to destroy Native American villages and recapture escaped fugitives.
- The American Colonization Society is founded with the purpose of resettling freed American blacks on the west coast of Africa. Few African Americans support the effort.
- Indiana, the nineteenth state, is admitted as a free state.
- Secretary of State James Monroe, another slaveholder and former governor of Virginia, is elected the fifth president.

# Chapter Five

# "MR. JEFFERSON'S PEOPLE"

# THE STORY OF ISAAC GRANGER

Nothing is more certainly written in the book of fate than that these people are to be free. Nor is it less certain that the two races, equally free, cannot live in the same government.
—THOMAS JEFFERSON, 1821

The British were coming.

It was an unusually cold day in January 1781. A small boy stood outside, watching as the red-coated soldiers marched into Richmond, Virginia.

The British lined up three cannons and fired.

"One of the cannon-balls knocked off the top of a butcher's house," the boy, Isaac Granger, recalled many years later. His

*Isaac Granger Jefferson in an 1845 daguerreotype, an early type of photograph, taken when he was about seventy years old.* [Unknown photographer / Tracy W. McGregor Library of American History, Special Collections, University of Virginia Library]

mother ran out and grabbed him by the hand, scurrying with him back into the kitchen. "In ten minutes not a white man was to be seen in Richmond. They ran as hard as they could."

One of those fleeing white men was Thomas Jefferson. "When they fired the cannon Old Master called out to John to fetch his horse Caractacus from the stable and rode off." About five years old at the time, Isaac was one of the youngest in a group of enslaved people who were in Richmond serving Thomas Jefferson, the man Isaac called "Old Master."

During the American Revolution, the author of the Declaration of Independence was elected governor of Virginia. Richmond had become Virginia's capital, but in 1781, it was little more than a country village with dirt streets, only two brick buildings, and modest wooden houses. With a market area of shops, churches, and taverns, it was home to about seven hundred residents, about half of whom were enslaved African Americans. They worked in town or on farms near this small tobacco trading post set among the rolling hills beside the James River.

On January 5, 1781, when the British reached the wood-frame townhouse where Thomas Jefferson was living, they found only some of Jefferson's enslaved servants. The governor of Virginia had already sent his own family to safety at a nearby plantation. His wife, Martha, and their three daughters—eight-year-old Patsy, two-year-old Polly, and a five-week-old baby, Lucy—were far from harm when the British soldiers arrived.

Under the command of Benedict Arnold, the notorious turncoat American general who now fought with the British, the men carried silver handcuffs meant for the author of the Declaration of Independence. An officer—perhaps even Benedict Arnold himself—demanded to know where Governor Jefferson was.

"He's gone to the mountains," replied George Granger, young Isaac's father. "The mountains" meant the mountainous region about seventy miles to the west. Monticello, which means "little mountain" in Italian, was Thomas Jefferson's plantation home, located on the top of a hill near the town of Charlottesville, Virginia.

But George Granger had lied. Jefferson was not far off; he was watching from a nearby hilltop as Virginia's capital fell. At dawn that day, Jefferson had tried to rally Virginia's militia to action. But it was hopeless. Many Virginians were unwilling to risk their lives and property. Others were afraid that their enslaved people would run away if they left to fight. The few who did show up fled at the sight of the British troops.

Helpless, Jefferson took off for the hills, barely escaping before the British burst into the house.

The British officer was disappointed. He was eager to arrest

Thomas Jefferson as a traitor to the king. Demanding the keys to the house, the officer asked where the silverware was.

"It was all sent up to the mountains," answered George Granger, once again deceiving the British officer. In fact, the household silver had been hidden, some around the kitchen and some in the bed ticking—the thick linen or cotton covering of a mattress.

As Isaac later told it, the British then ransacked the house. They found the cellar where Jefferson kept his best rum and finest wines, breaking the necks off the bottles with their swords. "Old Master had plenty of wine and rum the best," Isaac recalled. "Used to have Antigua rum, twelve years old." The British soldiers fed corn to their horses and took meat, cattle, sheep, and hogs.

After taking over the mostly abandoned capital, British soldiers went off to search nearby farms, still trying to hunt down Jefferson. Without finding their prey, the soldiers returned and set about looting Richmond. Shops and houses were emptied of tobacco, sugar, molasses, sailcloth, and coffee—anything of value. Many of the British troops found rum and wine and got drunk.

A few days later, the British marched out of Richmond, carrying the spoils of war. Food, alcohol, and the rest of their loot were piled into about a dozen wagons before they put a torch to the town and nearby farms.

Fanned by strong winds, the fires reduced Richmond to ashes. The British soldiers took something else of great value. They gathered some of "Mr. Jefferson's people" as captives. Young Isaac, his mother, his father, and a handful of others were marched away, the smallest children loaded in wagons.

Isaac remembered the day vividly. Though he must have been terrified at being ripped from all that was familiar to him, his later description made it sound almost like an adventure. He recounted British soldiers teasing a small boy even as they took care of him. He described how one of the officers gave him a drum to beat, nicknamed him Sambo, and fed him bread and meat. The officer also "put a cocked hat on [my] head and a red coat . . . and all laughed. [The] coat a monstrous great big thing: when [I] was in it, couldn't see nothing of it but the sleeves dangling down."

Besides Isaac and his parents, the group of captives included Jupiter, Jefferson's longtime valet who had become his carriage driver; Jupiter's wife, a cook named Sukey; seamstress Mary Hemings, a member of Monticello's large Hemings family; and a few other small children—Molly, Daniel, Joe, and Wormley.

Walking beside the wagons, each guarded by ten soldiers, the group left Richmond and crossed a river in small boats. Many enslaved people taken from other nearby farms joined them.

As the captives moved south with the British troops, Isaac could hear the far-off sounds of war. Gunfire and cannons boomed in the distance. As frightening as the sights and sounds around Isaac must have been, perhaps even more terrifying for his parents was the uncertainty. Would they see Monticello again? What would the feared redcoats do with them? But as they made the journey toward an unknown fate, some things did not change. Isaac's mother, Ursula, for example, served new masters—she was forced to cook and do laundry for the British captors.

Although the British may have been a frightening enemy to some, others may have seen the redcoats as liberators. Early in the war for independence, many of Virginia's enslaved people believed that freedom was possible. Their hopes had been born in November 1775, a few months after the Revolution began. In a proclamation, the British governor general of Virginia, John Murray, Earl of Dunmore, announced that slaves or indentured servants who left their owners to fight with the British would be freed.

Dunmore's Proclamation shook white Virginia to its core. In states like Virginia that had large enslaved communities, few things were more terrifying to white people—whether or not

*Dunmore's Proclamation, issued November 7, 1775, promised freedom to slaves who fled their masters.* [Library of Congress, Rare Book and Special Collections Division, rbpe 178018ob]

By His Excellency the Right Honorable JOHN Earl of DUNMORE, His MAJESTY's Lieutenant and Governor General of the Colony and Dominion of VIRGINIA, and Vice Admiral of the same.

# A PROCLAMATION.

AS I have ever entertained Hopes, that an Accommodation might have taken Place between GREAT-BRITAIN and this Colony, without being compelled by my Duty to this most disagreeable but now absolutely necessary Step, rendered so by a Body of armed Men unlawfully assembled, firing on His MAJESTY's Tenders, and the formation of an Army, and that Army now on their March to attack His Majesty's Troops and destroy the well disposed Subjects of this Colony. To defeat such treasonable Purposes, and that all such Traitors, and their Abettors, may be brought to Justice, and that the Peace, and good Order of this Colony may be again restored, which the ordinary Course of the Civil Law is unable to effect; I have thought fit to issue this my Proclamation, hereby declaring, that until the aforesaid good Purposes can be obtained, I do in Virtue of the Power and Authority to ME given, by His MAJESTY, determine to execute Martial Law, and cause the same to be executed throughout this Colony: and to the end that Peace and good Order may the sooner be restored, I do require every Person capable of bearing Arms, to resort to His MAJESTY's STANDARD, or be looked upon as Traitors to His MAJESTY's Crown and Government, and thereby become liable to the Penalty the Law inflicts upon such Offences; such as forfeiture of Life, confiscation of Lands, &c. &c. And I do hereby further declare all indented Servants, Negroes, or others, (appertaining to Rebels,) free that are able and willing to bear Arms, they joining His MAJESTY's Troops as soon as may be, for the more speedily reducing this Colony to a proper Sense of their Duty, to His MAJESTY's Crown and Dignity. I do further order, and require, all His MAJESTY's Leige Subjects, to retain their Quitrents, or any other Taxes due or that may become due, in their own Custody, till such Time as Peace may be again restored to this at present most unhappy Country, or demanded of them for their former salutary Purposes, by Officers properly authorised to receive the same.

GIVEN under my Hand on board the Ship WILLIAM, off NORFOLK, the 7th Day of NOVEMBER, in the SIXTEENTH Year of His MAJESTY's Reign.

DUNMORE.

(GOD save the KING.)

they owned slaves—than the idea of a violent uprising of slaves. The idea that tens of thousands of people who labored, cooked meals, and ran households could rise up and leave—or worse—was a nightmare.

Dunmore's Proclamation actually pushed many slave-holders who were on the fence about supporting the rebellion over to the patriot side. The Revolution is often presented as a war for freedom and liberty and to rid America of tyrannical colonial taxes. That proud image ignores the role that slavery played in influencing some people's attitudes about the war. The very real fear that the British would free America's enslaved people was as important as a shipload of tea or a slogan such as "No taxation without representation."

The number of enslaved people who took up Dunmore's offer was small—a few hundred to possibly two thousand. Some of them joined what Dunmore called the Ethiopian Regiment, a force that ended up weakened by yellow fever, attacked by patriot soldiers, and chased from Virginia. While Dunmore's liberated black fighters had not won any battles, they left behind angry slaveholders.

But a larger exodus of runaways was to come. In 1779, Henry Clinton, the British commander in chief in America, again issued an offer of freedom. It was not done out of the goodness of his heart—and the offer came with some fine print. Only the *rebellious patriots* would lose their slaves. Those Americans remaining loyal to the king—known as Tories—could keep their servants and laborers. Clinton thought that freeing the patriots' slaves would weaken their armies and the American will to fight.

Clinton was partly right. The British swept through Georgia, the Carolinas, and into Virginia, and they met little resistance as the war continued in 1781. And with each British victory, more African Americans deserted farms and plantations in what has been called the "largest slave uprising in our history."

Surely some of the people from Jefferson's Monticello knew of the British promise. But what did they make of it? Was it a trick? Would they be made slaves to the British?

The people taken from Richmond eventually reached a place Isaac called "Little York"—better known now as Yorktown. By the summer of 1781, Isaac and the rest of Jefferson's enslaved people had joined thousands of African Americans in this small tobacco port on the Chesapeake Bay. The British army had moved there, led by General Charles Cornwallis.

General Cornwallis still wanted Jefferson. Thinking he had another chance to capture the patriot leader in May 1781, Cornwallis dispatched Major Banastre Tarleton and a company of horsemen to hunt down Jefferson once more. Feared and hated by Americans, Tarleton had a reputation for cruelty. After one battle, in a grotesque breach of the accepted rules of war, he had ordered the massacre of surrendering French and American soldiers.

Obsessed with capturing one of the most notorious traitors to the king, Tarleton and his mounted troops raced at full speed for Charlottesville and Monticello. As they closed in, a Virginia militiaman galloped all night to warn Jefferson. From the heights of Monticello, Jefferson watched the British troops through his spyglass, or hand telescope. After once more sending his family to safety, Jefferson again slipped through his enemy's fingers, minutes before the British arrived.

The British horsemen who thundered up the mountain were

*Thomas Jefferson's hand telescope, likely used to see the British soldiers who were coming for him in May 1781.* [Thomas Jefferson Foundation at Monticello]

frustrated—Jefferson had again escaped their handcuffs. But the British would not leave empty-handed. As they had in Richmond in January, they took enslaved people from Monticello, along with some others from Jefferson's nearby Elk Hill and Willis Creek farms. Some of these people went willingly, thinking that they might be freed. All were eventually marched off to Yorktown, where Cornwallis's army of some 8,000 soldiers was camped.

By summertime, Cornwallis had put many of the African American refugees to work in Yorktown, digging trenches and building fortifications. Others cooked, did laundry, and cut wood. Hard labor. Backbreaking work. Long hours in the Virginia summer heat. If this was freedom under the British, it must have seemed no different from slavery.

As Cornwallis waited for guns, supplies, and men to arrive by sea from New York, all the people in Yorktown suffered. Poorly dressed and malnourished, they faced lethal diseases like dysentery, smallpox, and typhus—epidemics typical in army camps where basic sanitation was poor and drinking water carried deadly germs. The heat and humidity of a Tidewater Virginia summer added to the toll.

As the months rolled by, Cornwallis grew desperate. Feeding and caring for his sick, hungry troops and the thousands of starving black people became impossible. There were too many mouths to feed and too little food. With supplies shrinking and his men dropping, Cornwallis coldly started to force many refugees out of the town. Yorktown's wretched scene grew grimmer. The nearby woods and roads were littered with the dead and dying.

As a witness to this turning point in American history, young Isaac Granger remembered it well. "It was very sickly at York," he recalled many years later. "Great many colored people died there."

In October 1781, General George Washington and his French allies finally surrounded Yorktown and trapped Cornwallis. As mortars and cannonballs smashed into every house and building, British soldiers and African American refugees—including little Isaac—cringed under the bombardment.

"Wallis [General Cornwallis] had a cave dug and was hid in there," Isaac remembered. "There was tremendous firing and smoke: seemed like heaven and earth was come together." Every time the great guns fired, Isaac said he jumped off the ground. He said he "heard the wounded men hollerin'. When the smoke blow off you see the dead men laying on the ground."

Cornwallis was forced to surrender on October 19, 1781, as described in the story of Billy Lee. The American Revolution was not officially over yet, but most of the fighting was done.

Isaac had survived the deadly battle and witnessed history. But Isaac's Yorktown saga did not end there. The five-year-old boy would have an encounter with the hero of Yorktown—the man who would become America's first president.

"General Washington brought all Mr. Jefferson's folks and about twenty of Tuckahoe Tom's [Thomas Mann Randolph's] back to Richmond with him," Isaac remembered. Washington then "sent word to Mr. Jefferson to send down to Richmond for his servants. Old Master sent down two wagons right away and all of 'em that was carried away went up back to Monticello. . . . Old Master was mightly pleased to see his people come back safe and sound."

It was a great day for the United States of America. The hard-fought war for the nation's freedom was over. Washington and Jefferson had secured independence from Great Britain. But the enslaved people at Mount Vernon and Monticello were still in bondage, along with the thousands of others who would be forced back into enslavement.

Some of the runaways and refugees in Yorktown suffered a fate worse than simply returning to their former plantations and homes. Many Virginia slaveholders were worried that those who had escaped had gotten a taste of freedom. Would they want more?

For many slaveholders, that possibility was too dangerous. Out of fear, or perhaps a desire to punish those who had escaped, some owners sold many of these recaptured African

Americans to new owners deeper South or in the West Indies, breaking up families forever.

Twenty-six people from Jefferson's properties had either been captured or went willingly with the British. Fifteen of them died of smallpox or other camp diseases. Some came back. Others were sold, including a young man named Robin who had escaped from Monticello. "Jefferson sold several young men with a propensity for running away," Monticello historian Lucia Stanton explains, "in accordance with his policy of ridding his domain of disruptive elements."

Six years of war had been hard on Monticello and much of Virginia. Starvation, disease, and death had all taken a toll. Still, at the end of the war, the home state of Washington, Jefferson, and Madison had actually increased its total number of enslaved people—there were 236,000 slaves in Virginia, up from 210,000 at the start of the war.

Among those thousands was young Isaac Granger. About six when he was returned to Monticello, he later provided a fascinating testimonial of surviving bombardments, starvation, and disease at Yorktown, then

*The west elevation of the main house at Monticello. The cabins of enslaved workers were nearby.* [Jack Looney / Thomas Jefferson Foundation at Monticello]

going on to see a great deal of Monticello's history long after the Revolution ended.

Isaac told his stories of life among "Mr. Jefferson's people" to the Reverend Charles Campbell, a white man from Petersburg who had been a lawyer, newspaper publisher, historian, and schoolteacher. Campbell met Isaac in Petersburg, Virginia, in the 1840s, when Isaac was in his seventies. Later, Campbell took Isaac to a shop to have a daguerreotype—a kind of early photograph—made in 1847. He wrote down Isaac's memories of life with Jefferson. Campbell described Isaac as "rather tall, of strong frame, stoops a little, in color ebony; sensible, intelligent, pleasant."

Like the recollections of anyone telling childhood stories from more than a half century earlier, Isaac's tales as Campbell recorded them must be treated for what they are— memories colored by time and many retellings. Historians try to separate tall tales and fanciful recollections from actual events. But many historians give weight to Isaac's stories. Other documents and sources have vouched for much of what he recalled. His remembrances are accepted as part of the record of Jefferson's life and relationships with the people who labored for his "happiness," as Jefferson once said of Monticello's enslaved workers.

\* \* \*

Like George Washington, Thomas Jefferson grew up in Virginia's elite world of plantation life. The third of ten children and the oldest boy, he was born on April 13, 1743, at Shadwell, the family plantation in Virginia's Piedmont region. His father, Peter Jefferson, was a well-to-do planter and his mother, Jane Randolph, came from another large, prominent Virginia family.

When Peter Jefferson died in 1757, his son Thomas was fourteen years old. His lands and estate were divided between Thomas and his younger brother Randolph. Thomas Jefferson inherited approximately 5,000 acres, including the Shadwell property and what would later become his Monticello estate. The land came with nearly forty slaves.

A boy named Jupiter was born in the same year as Thomas Jefferson. The two boys grew up together, swimming and fishing in the Virginia countryside. When they turned twenty-one, however, their lives and relationship changed permanently. Jupiter was black and born enslaved. He went from being Thomas Jefferson's childhood playmate to becoming his personal servant—which meant, in Jefferson's words, to "shave, dress and follow me on horseback."

Now master and slave instead of boyhood friends, Jupiter rode beside Jefferson, buying his books and fiddle strings, paying his bills, and even lending him money, "to provide tips to other slaves, the domestic servants of his Williamsburg friends." He was Jefferson's trusty servant, permitted to travel alone with important papers or to collect money that was owed to Jefferson.

*Master and slave. Trusty servant. Black and white.* Simple words, but life and history are never simply black and white. Jefferson's relationships with Jupiter and the other people he legally owned would prove that—and so do his actions regarding slavery. In 1769, he introduced a bill in Virginia's legislature that would have allowed slaveholders to free their enslaved people. The bill was defeated. In a legal case he argued a year later, Jefferson said that his mixed-race client should be free because "every one comes into the world with a right to his own person, which includes the liberty of moving and using it at his own will." He lost the case.

About the same time, however, Jefferson advertised in *The Virginia Gazette* for the return of an enslaved mulatto shoemaker named Sandy. The man had escaped from Monticello, taking a white horse with him. Describing Sandy, Jefferson noted, "He is greatly addicted to drink, and when drunk is insolent and disorderly, in his conversation he swears much, and in his behavior is artful and knavish." Jefferson offered a reward of forty shillings for his return. Sandy was returned and sold within three years.

Here is America's great contradiction. Jefferson wrote about the ideals and principles of equality and even proposed some small steps toward ending American slavery. But he also owned people and was completely dependent on them for his livelihood and personal comfort until the day he died. Is this simply hypocrisy—saying one thing but doing another? Or is it more complicated?

Jefferson's fortunes took a great leap when he, like George Washington, married a wealthy widow. On New Year's Day in 1772, Jefferson married twenty-three-year-old Martha Wayles Skelton, daughter of John Wayles, an immigrant from England who had become a wealthy farmer, lawyer, and slave trader. They made the one-hundred-mile trip from her father's home to Jefferson's plantation in one of the worst snowstorms in Virginia history.

Martha Jefferson was said to be a beautiful woman, although there were no known portraits made during her life. She was educated and loved to read, like Jefferson. And, like Jefferson, Martha was a musician. She played the guitar and other instruments in duets with her husband, a passionate violinist. To all who saw the couple, including Monticello's enslaved people, Martha and Thomas Jefferson made a loving match.

A year and a half after they married, John Wayles died. In 1773, Thomas and Martha Jefferson inherited 135 enslaved people and 11,000 acres of property from Wayles. This large estate included the enslaved family of Betty Hemings.

A mixed-race woman born in 1735, Betty was the daughter of

an enslaved African woman whose name is not known for certain and a white ship's captain named Hemings. In the Wayles house, Betty Hemings came to occupy a position that few enslaved women attained.

In 1748, the first wife of John Wayles died just weeks after giving birth to a daughter, Martha Wayles. As a house servant, the teenage Betty Hemings would have been responsible for taking care of the infant girl. Betty became a mother figure for Martha.

Wayles remarried twice, and following the death of his third wife in 1761, Betty Hemings—now in her twenties—became Wayles's "concubine." At the time, the term was used to mean an unmarried woman who may live with a man but is not the legal or social equal of a wife—similar to the modern word *mistress*.

Over the course of eleven years, Betty had six children with John Wayles. But as the children of an enslaved woman, they were enslaved. One of them, born in 1773, was a girl named Sarah. Called Sally, she was Martha Jefferson's half sister— and would one day play a significant role in Thomas Jefferson's life.

After John Wayles died, the entire Hemings family moved to Monticello. There is no record of what Martha Jefferson thought of having a half sister who was forced to be her servant. It was like the fairy tale "Cinderella," in which some sisters are treated well while one must do the housework. But this was no fairy tale, and in the tragic world of American slavery, it was far from unusual. "It is only through piercing the veil of southern society's laws, including its fictions about family," says historian Annette Gordon-Reed, "that we can take the first step toward getting at the reality of black and white lives under slavery."

At his wife's request, Jefferson purchased other people. In 1773, he bought Ursula Granger, known for her talents as a skillful cook, along with her children, Bagwell and George (called "Little George"). In a separate auction, Jefferson purchased "Big" (or "Great") George Granger. Although George and Ursula Granger were not legally married—legal marriage was for whites only—they considered themselves husband and wife. Unlike some slaveholders, Jefferson recognized their relationship and helped to unite them at Monticello, where Isaac was born in 1775.

In the remarkable year of 1776, Thomas Jefferson wrote the Declaration of Independence, including those timeless words *All men are created equal*. That same year, he recorded a census of the "Number of souls in my family." The total was 117, and it included his wife, daughters, sixteen freemen—overseers and other paid workmen—and eighty-three slaves.

Enslaved people living in close quarters with slave owners made for close relationships. Just how close can be seen in the story Isaac told of Jefferson's first daughter, Martha, known as Patsy. Born in 1772, Patsy was in poor health until Isaac's mother, Ursula, nursed her. A wet nurse is a woman who is lactating—producing breast milk—and feeds another woman's baby. Ursula Granger had given birth to a boy named Archy, who later died. According to a letter written by Jefferson, Patsy "recovered almost instantaneously by a good breast of milk."

As a boy doing small chores, Isaac Granger witnessed the plantation's daily routines. He recalled Mrs. Jefferson reading aloud from a "cookery book" to his mother, giving instructions on how to make cakes and tarts. He also recalled the many inventions and labor-saving gadgets, some designed by Jefferson, that filled the redbrick house modeled on the classical designs of Andrea Palladio, a renowned Italian architect.

One of Jefferson's most famous designs was a revolving bookstand that allowed him to keep several books open at once as he worked. Isaac also remembered what he called Jefferson's "copyin' machine," or polygraph, which could automatically produce an exact copy of what Jefferson wrote with his own pen.

Another innovation was the dumbwaiter, which moved hot food and bottles of wine from the belowground kitchens and storerooms—called "dependencies"—up to the first floor. "When he wanted anything he had nothin' to do but turn a

*Jefferson's revolving bookstand, one of his inventions.*
[Thomas Jefferson's Foundation at Monticello]

crank and the dumb-waiter would bring him water or fruit on a plate or anything he wanted," Isaac remembered.

Modern visitors to Monticello marvel at its beauty and Jefferson's genius. But a visitor to Monticello was once struck by the "unpleasant contrast" between this elegant home—a

*Jefferson's polygraph, given to him by inventor John Isaac Hawkins, made copies of letters and documents, circa 1806.* [University of Virginia]

"palace," as he called it—and the slave dwellings beside it. At Monticello, several enslaved servants lived in underground rooms with stone walls and brick floors, near the dependencies beneath the first floor of the main house.

Most household servants, including the Grangers, lived in small log cabins in the shadow of Jefferson's great home, on what was called Mulberry Row (or Mulberry Lane or Mulberry Walk) for the pairs of mulberry trees planted there. Ursula Granger ruled the kitchen and other dependencies, supervising the cooking and washing, the smokehouse where meats were cured, and the cider-making operation.

*The interior of a reconstructed slave cabin at Monticello.* [Author's collection]

The area was the center of daily life at Monticello, with more than twenty one-room houses and workshops. Some of the servants worked the gardens there, which provided Jefferson's kitchen with fresh vegetables, herbs, and fruits.

Mulberry Row's small houses were between twelve and fourteen feet wide and fourteen to twenty feet long, with dirt floors and a fireplace. Although far from decent living conditions by today's standards, these cabins were actually better than typical slave dwellings of the period. The field hands who worked the tobacco and wheat fields lived in much rougher slave quarters closer to the fields, where they labored long hours in all weather, all year.

Thomas Jefferson loved the finer things in life, like good wines and food cooked in the French style. Monticello's enslaved

*The gardens beside Mulberry Row at Monticello provided food for the Jefferson family.* [Author's collection]

people had a different menu. Every cabin had a poultry yard and small vegetable garden. That helped the enslaved families get along with their weekly ration of cornmeal and a pound of pork.

Clothing was also strictly doled out. Each worker typically received two outfits a year—cotton for the summer and a mixture of cotton and wool for winter. A striped blanket was issued every three years.

For Monticello's enslaved people, there were really two working shifts. By day, servants did all the household work and field hands labored with the crops. At night, they had to work for themselves. "A second working day began after dark," says historian Lucia Stanton. "Mothers had to attend to their households, preparing meals, repairing clothing, and caring for their children." Men often hunted and trapped for food and to earn a little money. Isaac Granger's brother Bagwell is mentioned in Jefferson's farm accounts, selling Jefferson skins, fish, duck, cucumbers, and watermelons.

Isaac Granger offered vivid pictures of the ties between servant and master, the intimate daily contacts they had with each other. Since Isaac often went with Jefferson when he hunted squirrels and partridge, or visited him in Monticello's library and workrooms, he saw glimpses of Jefferson as the gentleman farmer and tinkerer. "My Old Master was as neat a hand as ever you see to make keys and locks and small chains. . . . He kept all kind of blacksmith and carpenter tools in a great case with shelves to it in his library."

Thomas Jefferson also loved music, according to Isaac. "Mr. Jefferson always singing when ridin' or walkin'. Hardly see him . . . out doors but what he was a-singin'," Isaac remembered. He "had a fine clear voice" and sang minuets and such and "fiddled in the parlor."

In September 1782, about a year after Isaac and the other Yorktown captives returned to Monticello, tragedy struck. At the age of thirty-three, Martha Jefferson died. In poor health since the birth of another daughter, Lucy, Jefferson's wife had been confined to bed, "dangerously ill" in Jefferson's words. This child was the second Jefferson girl named Lucy; the first had died in April 1781, a few months after the escape from Richmond.

A man deeply in love, Jefferson was stunned at the loss. By all accounts, he made his wife a deathbed promise that he would never marry again. According to Isaac, Jefferson didn't leave his bedroom for three weeks after the funeral, and then he spent weeks riding in circles around the grounds of Monticello. By his own words, Jefferson was nearly mad with grief. "This miserable kind of existence is really too burdensome to be borne," he wrote to a friend, sounding almost suicidal. Out of a sense of duty to his surviving children—Patsy (Martha), Polly (Mary), and Lucy—his Virginia neighbors, and finally his country, Jefferson came around. Getting a grip on his emotions, he resolved to become active in the nation's affairs again.

In 1784, Jefferson was appointed America's minister, or ambassador, to France. He left for Paris, taking along his oldest daughter, Patsy, and nineteen-year-old James Hemings, one of Betty's children. Jefferson wanted James trained to cook in the French style. Polly and Lucy were left behind with their aunt, Jefferson's sister-in-law.

While he was in Paris, tragedy struck again, and Jefferson received word that Lucy had died of whooping cough (also called pertussis). In addition to his wife, Martha, who had died after this Lucy was born, four of the six Jefferson children born to Martha had died in infancy or childhood: the two girls named Lucy, a girl named Jane, and an unnamed son. Only two of their children, Patsy and Polly, lived to adulthood.

In May 1787, nine-year-old Polly sailed to join her father and sister in Paris. It may seem difficult to believe, but Polly was sent on a long ocean voyage accompanied only by another girl just a few years older. Polly's traveling companion was Sally Hemings, a fourteen-year-old servant, another of Betty's children. After crossing the Atlantic, the two girls stopped in

London, where John Adams, the American minister to England, and his wife, Abigail, met the pair.

The girls went on to Paris, where Jefferson was reunited with his younger daughter, and Sally, with her brother. By this point, James Hemings had been Jefferson's valet and traveling attendant for years. Now he was learning gourmet cooking from French chefs and pastry cooks in a Parisian hotel. While there, James Hemings was also given a salary, part of which he used to take lessons in French from a tutor. One lesson he learned was that France had ended slavery. James was legally free there. He could have remained in France, or even returned to America as a free man. But he stayed with Jefferson. Some historians believe that James discussed his eventual freedom, which was granted in 1796, while in France with Jefferson.

There are no pictures of his sister Sally—no paintings or daguerreotypes as there would be of Isaac Granger one day. According to family accounts and traditions, Sally also resembled her late half sister, Martha Jefferson. There are only four descriptions of Sally on record. Jefferson's grandson described her as "light colored and decidedly good looking." But Isaac provided one vivid memory of her. "Sally [was] mighty near white.... Folks said that these Hemingses was old Mr. Wayles' children. Sally was very handsome: long straight hair down her back."

When Sally Hemings returned from Paris, she may have been pregnant, meaning her first child was conceived while she was a teenager in Paris. Sally's son Madison later said the child was born at Monticello but died soon after. Over the next few years, Sally remained at Monticello while Jefferson moved to New York to join the Washington administration. She would stay there for years, caring for Jefferson's private rooms and wardrobe. "He trusted her," wrote biographer Jon Meacham, "with the things he valued most."

For more than two centuries, people have claimed that Thomas Jefferson was the father of Sally's six children, four of whom lived to adulthood. The rumor of Jefferson's relationship with Sally Hemings first became public in 1802, when journalist James T. Callender published the charge.

Since then, and for many years after, Jefferson's family members, his biographers, and other defenders denied that Jefferson was the father of Sally's children. Many of them claimed that other men, possibly Jefferson's nephews, might have been the fathers of these children.

Recent scientific evidence, such as DNA testing, confirms that Jefferson or some male in his family fathered the children of Sally Hemings. Records also show that Jefferson was at Monticello during the times Sally Hemings was likely to have conceived her children. The combination of scientific evidence, documents, and oral traditions have convinced most people that Thomas Jefferson was the father of Sally's children, and it is now accepted as fact at Monticello.

The personal tragedies and controversies in Thomas Jefferson's life played out as America entered a new era of nationhood. When George Washington was elected the first president and took office in New York in 1789, John Adams became vice president and Jefferson was named the first secretary of state. Then in 1790, when the national capital was moved to Philadelphia, Jefferson moved, too. Like President Washington, he took enslaved people with him. One of them was Isaac Granger.

Now about fifteen years old—too young to be emancipated under Pennsylvania law—Isaac was apprenticed to a tinsmith, a Philadelphia Quaker. He began learning to make household items like plates and pots. After a week's time, he could make pepper boxes and graters from scraps of tin. Then he moved on to making tin cups.

After four years in Philadelphia learning his trade, Isaac was an accomplished tinsmith. Seeing Isaac's ability, Jefferson decided to send him back to Monticello to start a tin shop at the plantation. Jefferson believed that slavery could not end until the plantation system was replaced by manufacturing

and enslaved African Americans could learn useful trades. Monticello's tin shop, however, was ultimately not profitable.

Jefferson also set up a nail factory to produce the nails used at Monticello and sell them for profit. Isaac worked there as well, alongside other boys as young as ten years old. Over the next few years, while Jefferson was in Monticello after his years as secretary of state, Isaac set the standard as a nail maker; he turned out one thousand pounds of nails in the first six months of 1796, by far the most at Monticello.

Although he had seen how black freemen lived in Philadelphia, Isaac resumed the regular life of plantation bondage. He and an enslaved woman named Iris fell in love and started a family, producing two boys, Squire and Joyce, and later a girl named Maria. Isaac's father, "Great George," was meanwhile made the overseer—the man who supervised the enslaved farmhands of Monticello. The job of overseer, typically given to a free white man, was an extraordinary position of trust for an enslaved man, especially as the "Master of Monticello" was about to embark on the next step in his famous life.

Chosen the third American president in 1801, Jefferson moved into the new executive mansion in the new capital of Washington. The presidential home would eventually become

*Isaac would have worked in a building similar to this reconstructed nail shop on Mulberry Row.* [Author's collection]

known as the White House. John Adams and his wife, Abigail, had been the first to occupy the building, which was still unfinished in November 1800 when the Adamses first moved in. Large and drafty, the plastered walls still wet, the house was called the "great castle" by Abigail Adams.

But the President's House was far from a king's palace. The laundry was hung indoors, and thirteen fireplaces were kept burning to warm the house and dry both the walls and the presidential family's wet breeches. The privy—the presidential outhouse—was outdoors, pretty much in full view of the public.

Something else was far more upsetting to Mrs. Adams about the mansion and the new capital being laid out around it. Both the city and the President's House were being built with enslaved labor. That disgusted Mrs. Adams, who had grown up with enslaved servants but had come to hate slavery. Like many traditional New Englanders who believed in the virtue of hard work and honest wages, she also thought that slavery was a poor way to get a job done.

After watching a dozen enslaved men laboring outside the future White House, Abigail Adams complained to her uncle in a letter, "Two of our hardy New England men would do as much work in a day as the whole 12." She added that the twelve men and the other enslaved people she saw each day were often "half fed, and destitute of

*An interpretation of the early design of the White House.*
[Library of Congress, Prints & Photographs Division, LC-DIG-ppmsca-23683]

clothing," while the owners who hired out these men did nothing but keep their wages.

*A portrait of Abigail Adams, wife of John Adams, the second president of the United States, painted by Gilbert Stuart.*
[National Gallery of Art]

When John and Abigail Adams moved out in March 1801 and Thomas Jefferson moved in, Isaac did not go with President Jefferson. Three years earlier, Isaac, along with his wife, Iris, and two sons, Squire and Joyce, had been given to Jefferson's daughter Polly and her husband. They were among thirty enslaved people given to the couple as part of Polly's dowry.

More changes lay ahead for Isaac. At some point, the legal ownership of Isaac's entire family was transferred to Jefferson's other son-in-law, Thomas Mann Randolph, the husband of older daughter Patsy. Working for the Randolphs as a blacksmith, Isaac remained with the family for many years. Although Isaac later called Thomas Randolph a "fine master," he never mentioned that Randolph had sold the couple's daughter, Maria, in 1818 to a Monticello overseer. Nor did he mention the fate of his wife and two sons. Did Randolph sell them also? The old records have been lost.

Isaac was silent about another shadowy episode among Monticello's enslaved people. After Isaac left Monticello, a strange illness swept through Mulberry Row. First Jupiter, Jefferson's longtime valet and driver, became sick and died in 1799. Not long after, Isaac's brother George and then his father also fell sick, and both died later that year. Finally, Ursula Granger also became ill with "constant puking and shortness of breath," as Jefferson's daughter Patsy described it. Jefferson summoned a physician but it was futile, and Isaac's mother, Ursula, died in April 1800.

All four of them had been treated by a black man from a neighboring county who probably used African folk medicines and was also described as a "Negroe conjurer." (*Conjurer* is a word for a magician.) Whether they died from their disease or the so-called cure they were given, their fates—and Isaac's silence about his family—remain unsolved mysteries.

A year later, Jefferson was on his way to the White House. Among the very few enslaved people who traveled with him to Washington from Monticello were young women who were to be trained to cook in the President's House and then return. While in the capital, President Jefferson's domestic help was made up of mostly paid servants, although some were enslaved local people who had been hired out. Jefferson wrote in 1804, "At Washington I prefer white servants, who, when they misbehave, can be exchanged [dismissed]."

One of the great crises of this period came from the Caribbean island of Saint-Domingue, now known as Haiti. On this French colony, an uprising of enslaved people had turned into a violent rebellion. Inspired by America's revolution, these enslaved people had overthrown their white oppressors in a long, murderous revolt.

A French army sent to put down the rebellion met with disaster. The French troops were wiped out by a combination of fierce fighting and an epidemic of deadly yellow fever. The loss of this army was a key reason that Emperor Napoleon decided to sell France's enormous possessions in North America—the territory called Louisiana. That real estate deal, sealed in 1803 during Jefferson's first term, doubled the size of America overnight.

But the acquisition of Louisiana would also add to a growing crisis over the future of slavery in America. Would slavery be permitted in this massive piece of North America and the new states that would eventually be created from it?

The existing slave states wanted any new territories to be admitted into the Union with slavery allowed. That would mean more land to be worked with slave labor. It would also add considerable political power to the slave states—each new state would get seats in Congress and electoral votes based on their enslaved population because of the three-fifths rule in the Constitution. That was the essence of what "slave power" meant.

In other words, the Louisiana Purchase, one of President Thomas Jefferson's greatest accomplishments, added dangerous fuel to the fire of slave state versus free state.

On the other hand, in 1807 President Jefferson signed the law that ended the foreign slave trade in America. Jefferson believed that ending the slave trade would ultimately end slavery, but he did not take into account the natural increase of America's enslaved people. In 1810, there were a little more than one million enslaved African Americans. That number grew to four million over the next fifty years.

During his life, Thomas Jefferson had written angry words denouncing the slave trade. He called it a "cruel war against human nature," though the drafting committee removed those words from his version of the Declaration of Independence. He had stood up for the rights of enslaved people as an attorney. He had worked for laws that would enable Virginians to free their slaves more easily. Jefferson had drafted the law to ban slavery in new territories in the northwest, the area west of Pennsylvania and north of the Ohio River.

When Jefferson died on July 4, 1826—the fiftieth anniversary of the adoption of the Declaration of Independence and the same day on which John Adams died—there were still hundreds of enslaved people on his properties. Neither Jefferson nor his heirs could afford to emancipate anyone besides the children of Sally Hemings. Many other Monticello people were later sold to pay down Jefferson's debts.

By the time Thomas Jefferson died, Isaac was long gone from Monticello. At some point, he was sold again to a family named Archer, who moved to Petersburg, nearer to Richmond—the scene of his childhood adventure with the British in 1781. Finally, nearing the age of sixty, Isaac was given his freedom on February 21, 1834. He was officially registered as a "Free man of Color."

From that time on, Isaac lived and worked in Petersburg, Virginia, then a booming tobacco, farm market, and slave-trading town that had become a center for some of the state's first railroad lines. Working as a blacksmith, Isaac paid taxes and, according to tax records, even hired enslaved helpers to work in his shop.

This is a strange twist on the complex world of confusing roles and identities that slavery created. A former enslaved man hires enslaved boys to work in his shop. Did he think about the boys' freedom?

*Thomas Jefferson wrote the epitaph on his grave marker at Monticello. It does not mention that he was president of the United States.* [Author's collection]

There are whole books devoted to Thomas Jefferson's writings and letters. But for the most part, there are only fragments and scraps of public records of the lives of people like Isaac Granger—beyond the remarkable but incomplete account he gave Charles Campbell.

The stories Isaac told Campbell did not appear for many years. Isaac's words were apparently being prepared for publication when Campbell died in 1876. Isaac's memories and reflections, as Campbell wrote them, were not published until 1951. But the stories he told have been confirmed by other scholars and researchers and used by many historians as a source on Jefferson's life ever since.

Isaac's stories reveal much about Jefferson and the world of Monticello's enslaved people. But they hide perhaps more. Isaac often described the people who held him in bondage as kind and decent. He speaks well of them. But are these his true thoughts and feelings?

Even as a free man in Virginia, Isaac lived under written laws that restricted the legal rights of free blacks and the code of unwritten rules that applied to black people. Even free African Americans had to be very careful not to insult or otherwise offend whites. Any perceived wrongdoing could be met with a whipping, beating, or worse. Perhaps Isaac admired and even loved Jefferson. But to say otherwise in his lifetime would have been daring if not foolish. The face that African Americans presented to the white world was not always the reality of their lives and souls.

Isaac Granger Jefferson, as he called himself and was widely known in his later years, died in 1846 at the age of seventy-one, a free man of color.

# SLAVERY IN AMERICA TIME LINE
## 1817–1828

**1817** Mississippi, the twentieth state, is admitted as a slave state.

**1818** Illinois, the twenty-first state, is admitted as a free state.

**1819**
- Florida is purchased from Spain.
- Alabama becomes the twenty-second state, a slave state.

**1820**
- In March, the Missouri Compromise is signed into law after a long and bitter debate. It allows for Maine to be admitted as the twenty-third state, a free state. Missouri will join the Union as the twenty-fourth state with slavery permitted in 1821. Under the law, slavery is prohibited in Louisiana Purchase territory north of a designated border.
- In the fourth national census, the U.S. population has reached 9,638,453 with a black population of 1,777,254. Of those, 1,538,022 are enslaved.

**1821**
- Mexico grants permission to three hundred American families to settle in the Mexican territory of Texas. Stephen F. Austin leads the first Americans to Texas in 1825.
- Missouri is admitted as the twenty-fourth state, with slavery allowed. There are now twelve slave states and twelve free states.
- The American Colonization Society purchases a site in West Africa to establish the Republic of Liberia as a haven for emancipated American enslaved people; its first settlement and later capital is named Monrovia, after President James Monroe.

**1822** Near Charleston, South Carolina, one of the largest planned slave rebellions is put down when the conspiracy is revealed; its leader, Denmark Vesey, formerly enslaved, is caught and executed along with more than thirty enslaved people.

**1824** After the presidential election of 1824 fails to produce a winner, the House of Representatives elects John Quincy Adams of Massachusetts as the sixth American president. The winner of the popular vote, Andrew Jackson, claims that the election is the result of a "corrupt bargain."

**1826** On July 4, the fiftieth anniversary of the adoption of the Declaration of Independence, both Thomas Jefferson and John Adams die.

**1827** • The state of New York abolishes slavery.
• *Freedom's Journal*, the first black-owned newspaper, begins publication in New York City.

**1828** War hero Andrew Jackson, a slaveholder who lives in Tennessee, is elected the seventh American president.

## CHAPTER SIX

# WHITE HOUSE, BLACK MAN

*A photograph of Paul Jennings, once the enslaved servant of James and Dolley Madison.* [The Estate of Sylvia Jennings Alexander and Montpelier]

# THE STORY OF PAUL JENNINGS

A large part of his men were tall, strapping negroes, mixed with white sailors and marines. Mr. Madison reviewed them just before the fight, and asked Com[modore] Barney if his "negroes would not run on the approach of the British?" "No, sir," said Barney, "they don't know how to run; they will die by their guns first."
—PAUL JENNINGS ON AFRICAN AMERICAN TROOPS IN THE WAR OF 1812

The two races cannot co-exist, both being free & equal.
—JAMES MADISON IN AN 1826 LETTER TO THE MARQUIS DE LAFAYETTE

The British were coming. Again.

It was late in August 1814—a new century and a new war. Panic was sweeping Washington. A British admiral had boasted that he would put a torch to America's capital and take the president hostage.

For the second time, America was at war with Great Britain. In June 1812, more than thirty years after the Yorktown battle that ended the Revolution, Congress had declared war on the British. Two years of halfhearted fighting had barely touched American soil. But in the spring of 1814, the British were closing in on Washington.

Just the same, life went on as usual at the White House on August 24, 1814.

"Mrs. Madison ordered dinner to be ready at 3," recalled Paul Jennings, the fifteen-year-old enslaved servant of President James Madison and his wife, Dolley. "I set the table myself, and brought up the ale, cider, and wine, and placed them in the coolers, as all the Cabinet and several military gentlemen and strangers were expected."

As young Paul Jennings prepared for this White House meal, America's military leaders refused to believe that the British would attack the nation's capital. They thought nearby Baltimore, with its fortified harbor and busy port, was the more likely target. But British Admiral Alexander Cochrane, whose brother had died at Yorktown, had a different opinion. Earlier in the war, Americans had burned towns in Canada. Hot for revenge, the admiral ordered his men to "destroy and lay waste" to American towns, sparing only unarmed civilians.

Five thousand battle-tested British soldiers had landed near Bladensburg, Maryland, a tobacco port about ten miles from

Washington. Standing between the British and the nearly defenseless capital was an American force of about the same size. Poorly equipped, with little training and less combat experience, the Americans had simple orders: hold their ground, or the British would have a quick march into the capital.

A few weeks before, another British admiral, George Cockburn, threatened to capture the president's wife, Dolley Madison, and parade her through London's streets as a war trophy. Tall and stately, a beauty with black curls, Dolley Madison had become famous for her fashionable outfits—exotic turbans and low-cut dresses in the French style. Guests flocked to the weekly gatherings called salons that she hosted when the White House was opened to all visitors.

By the summer of 1814,

*Gilbert Stuart painted this portrait of Dolley Madison in 1804, five years before she became First Lady. By the time James Madison was president, his wife was an American celebrity, famed for her beauty and stylish fashions—a stark contrast to earlier First Ladies, who kept a much lower profile.* [White House Historical Association]

Dolley Madison's lavish White House parties had given way to the harsh realities of war. The British were closing in. But the Madisons had chosen not to run. Facing down the threat, they stayed at the White House, where one hundred men guarded the mansion and some cannons were placed at the entry gate.

As the tension grew, Paul Jennings watched. Born enslaved at Madison's Montpelier plantation in 1799, he was the son of a house servant and a white English merchant named Jennings. Paul Jennings spent his earliest years doing small chores—"a boy under his mother's feet in the big house enlisted as errand runner." He also served—and probably played with—Todd Payne, Dolley's son from her first marriage. Seven years older than Paul Jennings, Todd Payne was two when his father and brother died in a yellow fever epidemic. After Madison married the widowed Dolley, they raised the boy at Montpelier.

In 1809, when Paul was about ten, James Madison became the fourth president, and Paul Jennings was taken to Washington. There is no evidence that Paul could read or write before going to the White House. Chances are, he learned from listening as Payne or a Madison nephew was tutored at Montpelier or the White House.

Paul had keen memories of the time. "The east room was not finished," he recalled many years later. "And Pennsylvania

Avenue was not paved, but was always in an awful condition from either mud or dust. The city was a dreary place."

Paul was fifteen when the winds of war reached Washington in 1814. He saw it all.

"On the 24th of August, sure enough, the British reached Bladensburg, and the fight began between 11 and 12," Jennings later recounted. "Even that very morning [Secretary of War] General Armstrong assured Mrs. Madison there was no danger."

Confident that his wife was safe, President Madison had set off for Bladensburg to see the American defenses for himself and to raise morale among the troops. Back at the White House, Dolley Madison spent the day watching from the windows, showing no sign of panic. She was unaware that the battle had begun by midday.

"Since sunrise I have been turning my spy glass in every direction," she wrote to her sister in a long letter begun the night before, "watching with unwearied anxiety, hoping to discern the approach of my dear husband and his friends; but, alas, I can descry only groups of military wandering in all directions, as if there was a lack of arms, or of spirit to fight for their own firesides!"

In spite of her worries, Mrs. Madison wanted the White House staff to carry on as usual. She called for the table to be readied for as many as forty guests when the president returned. Paul Jennings finished setting out the silver and cold drinks. Then with the arrival of a frantic message, Jennings remembered, everything changed.

"As Sukey, the house-servant, was lolling out of a chamber window, James Smith, a free colored man who had accompanied Mr. Madison to Bladensburg, gallopped up to the house, waving his hat, and cried out, 'Clear out, clear out! General Armstrong has ordered a retreat!'"

This shock was followed by worse news. The Americans had suffered a humiliating defeat. Many of the American soldiers had simply abandoned their cannons, broken ranks, and run at the first sign of a British charge. The newspapers later mockingly called this chaotic retreat from battle the "Bladensburg Races" because men raced away from the front lines. The road to Washington was wide open.

The relative calm inside the White House soon turned to panic. Dolley Madison ordered the staff to evacuate. Almost defenseless, the White House was now a big bull's-eye.

Calling for her carriage, Dolley Madison rushed through the dining room. She had no idea what had become of President Madison. Gathering "what silver she could crowd into her old-fashioned reticule"—a handbag with a drawstring—she "then jumped into the chariot with her servant girl Sukey," said Paul Jennings. The British were expected in a few minutes.

As the crisis unfolded, Commodore Joshua Barney

commanded a group of small American gunboats—called a flotilla—to fend off the British warships. Forced to abandon their gunboats, the sailors became artillerymen manning the defenses on land at Bladensburg.

"A large part of his men were tall, strapping negroes, mixed with white sailors and marines," Paul Jennings later reported. "Mr. Madison reviewed them just before the fight,

*A portrait of President James Madison by Gilbert Stuart.* [White House Historical Association]

and asked Com[modore] Barney if his 'negroes would not run on the approach of the British?' 'No, sir,' said Barney, 'they don't know how to run; they will die by their guns first.'"

These men fought hard until they were killed or captured, and the British took Barney prisoner. Those black sailors who fought and died were heroic. But in the patriotic paintings of the War of 1812, the African American sailors-turned-soldiers are mostly missing—one more example of being left in the shadows of history.

*Commodore Joshua Barney, a naval hero in both the Revolution and the War of 1812. He was wounded and captured at Bladensburg, and the bullet wound he received that day is believed to have been responsible for his death in 1816.*

Among Barney's crew was Charles Ball, a young man from Maryland who had escaped his enslavement and told navy recruiters he was free. Eager for any volunteers, they were happy to sign him up. Ball fearlessly helped defend the nation's capital even as white militiamen fled.

While Barney's mixed-race unit fought heroically, another group of African Americans had sided with the opposition. Among the British troops that day was a company of the Corps of Colonial Marines—a unit made up of African Americans also fighting for their freedom. During the earlier American Revolution, the British offered emancipation to enslaved people who came to their side. They again called for African Americans to join their ranks during the War of 1812. Thousands took the chance to win freedom; as many as

3,400 enslaved people from Maryland and Virginia fled to British ships.

Following the rout at Bladensburg, the British halted their march, pausing to recover in the late August heat. While the British rested, a group of Washington locals, later described by Paul Jennings as "rabble," took the opportunity to ransack the White House. "People were running in every direction," he recalled, as townspeople grabbed what they could and loaded wagons. In the chaos, these American looters, according to Jennings, "stole lots of silver and whatever they could lay their hands on."

In the frenzy, a prized portrait

*Charles Ball escaped slavery to fight in the War of 1812 but would later be reenslaved.* [National Park Service]

of George Washington was also taken from the White House. This cherished treasure was a nearly life-size painting that showed Washington standing in a simple black suit. With one hand on a sword and the other outstretched in a gesture of peace, it was a picture of a modest man—not an all-conquering hero—as he rejected calls for a third term in office.

A popular legend grew that Dolley Madison had cut the portrait out of its huge, heavy frame with a carving knife and carried it away. Paul Jennings offered a different account.

"This is totally false," he claimed many years later. "She had no time for doing it. It would have required a ladder to get it down. All she carried off was the silver in her reticule, as the British were thought to be but a few squares off. . . . John Susé . . . and Magraw, the President's gardener, took it down and sent it off on a wagon, with some large silver urns and such other valuables as could be hastily got hold of."

Dolley Madison had asked two men who were passing by to safeguard the painting. They hid it in a Maryland barn until it was eventually returned to the White House, where it still hangs. Art experts determined many years later that the ornate frame of the painting was actually broken to get the canvas.

*This Gilbert Stuart portrait of George Washington was rescued in August 1814. It was later returned to the White House, where it still hangs.* [White House Historical Association]

Several hours after Dolley fled, President Madison arrived safely back at the mostly deserted White House. With the British army moving in and a violent thunderstorm brewing, Madison decided that remaining in the capital was out of the question. He and his aides were ferried across the Potomac River to Virginia.

Among the last to leave the mansion were Paul Jennings and John Sioussat, the White House steward and doorkeeper whom Jennings called "Susé." Known as French John, he carried away Dolley Madison's bird, a prized macaw, and left her beloved pet safely at the French ambassador's residence.

When the British troops finally entered Washington that evening, their plan was clear. They were going to destroy Washington's official buildings in revenge for the Americans' burning of the town of York (now Toronto) in Canada earlier in the war.

Making an enormous bonfire out of the mahogany chairs used by Congress, the British troops set fire to the Capitol building. The Library of Congress collection was also destroyed, with some 3,000 books going up in flames. (The library's collection was later rebuilt with books purchased from Thomas Jefferson's library.)

The British troops moved on to the empty White House. Exhausted from the battle and the march, the British officers found the table set, just as Paul Jennings had left it.

"Several kinds of wine, in handsome cut glass decanters, were cooling on the sideboard," one British officer reported later. "Plate holders stood by the fireplace, filled with dishes and plates; knives, forks and spoons were arranged for immediate use; in short, everything was ready for the entertainment of a ceremonious party."

Enjoying this presidential feast, the British officers were in a giddy mood. One of them put Madison's tricorner hat on the point of a bayonet and said if they could not capture "the little president," they could still parade his hat through London. Another officer took a cushion from a chair and joked that it would help him "warmly recall Mrs. Madison's seat."

Then the White House was set afire. Furniture was piled in the center of rooms, and oil-soaked rags were lit and tossed through broken windows. Bystanders watched as the mansion was engulfed in flames, lighting up the night sky. As one witness described it, "the heavens redden'd with the blaze!"

Wandering the fallen city's streets, Paul Jennings watched Washington burn. "I heard a tremendous explosion, and, rushing out, saw that the public buildings, navy yard, ropewalks, &c., were on fire."

The commander of the United States Navy Yard had ordered the buildings and warships there to be destroyed to prevent

[NEXT PAGES] *This wood engraving depicts the capture and burning of Washington in August 1814.* [Library of Congress, Prints & Photographs Division, cph 3c17176]

their capture. As the explosions Jennings heard shook the city, it must have seemed like the end of the world.

A powerful thunderstorm finally broke the summer night, and the torrential rains doused the flames. But the damage was done. All that remained of the President's House was a burned shell.

A few days after the British left the city, James Madison and his wife returned to the smoldering, ruined capital with Paul Jennings and the other servants. They moved into a temporary home as peace talks took place in Paris. The treaty ending the War of 1812 was reached on Christmas Eve 1814, and the good news arrived in Washington early in 1815.

"We were crazy with joy," Paul Jennings remembered. Butler John Freeman served wine to everyone, including the ser-

vants. Paul Jennings grabbed an instrument and added to the celebration. "I played the President's March on the violin, John Susé

*From the White House, a piece of wood charred by the fire of 1814.* [Smithsonian Museum of American History]

*An architectural drawing of plans for the restored White House, 1817.*
[Library of Congress, Prints & Photographs Division, LC-DIG-ppmsca-09502]

and some others were drunk for two days, and such another joyful time was never seen in Washington. Mr. Madison and all his Cabinet were as pleased as any, but did not show their joy in this manner."

While some of the servants may have had a bit too much to drink that day, Jennings said that the president did not join them. James Madison was very "temperate in his habits." Jennings remembered, "I don't think he drank a quart of brandy in his whole life.... When he had hard drinkers at his table, who had put away his choice Madeira pretty freely, in response to their numerous toasts, he would just touch the glass to his lips, or dilute it with water, as they pushed about the decanters. For the last fifteen years of his life he drank no wine at all."

The reconstruction of the White House took more than three years; Madison would never live there again. It was only finished in time for his successor, James Monroe, the fifth president.

Elected in 1816, Monroe was another slaveholding Virginia neighbor of Jefferson and Madison who would bring enslaved people to Washington. And when the White House officially reopened to the public on New Year's Day 1818, the restored mansion—like the original—had been built with slave labor.

After President James Madison's second term ended in March 1817, the Madisons returned to Montpelier, their estate in Orange, Virginia. Paul Jennings, Dolley's maid Sukey—whose full name was Susan Edwards—and the other Madison enslaved people went back with them. For James Madison and Paul Jennings both, it was a return to their birthplace.

With two eventful terms over, the former president wanted nothing more than the quiet life of Montpelier. Eight years in office and a war had taken their toll on an aging James Madison. Paul Jennings, now about eighteen years old, was shifted from house servant to body servant. His new duties included shaving and dressing the former president and traveling with him. "I was always with Mr. Madison till he died, and shaved him every other day for sixteen years," Jennings later said.

Born on March 16, 1751, James Madison had grown up on this large plantation with a sweeping view of Virginia's Blue Ridge Mountains. The property had first belonged to James Madison's grandfather, Ambrose Madison, who moved his wife and three children there in 1732 and called the estate Mount Pleasant. Later its name was changed to Montpelier.

In August 1732, soon after arriving, Ambrose Madison became ill and died in mysterious circumstances. Three enslaved people—Pompey, Dido, and Turk—were quickly convicted of poisoning Ambrose Madison.

Pompey, who was being leased to Madison by a neighboring planter, was executed by hanging. But Turk, a man, and Dido, a woman, received lesser sentences—twenty-nine lashes each—since their role in the plot was not fully proved.

Dido and Turk remained at the plantation with Ambrose's widow, Frances Madison; her oldest son, James (father of the future president); and two other children. In other words, James Madison's grandmother and his father spent much of

*The view west to the mountains of Virginia from the Montpelier home of James Madison.* [Author's collection]

their lives with two people who may have conspired to kill Ambrose Madison.

The future president, the younger James Madison, left home for school in New Jersey—the college would later be called Princeton—in 1769. A young man about Madison's age named Sawney went with him. But Sawney did not go as a student; he was enslaved. He stayed there briefly, sleeping on the floor outside Madison's room, before returning to Montpelier to spend the rest of his life in the tobacco fields.

Madison had grown up with the idea that slaves might kill their masters. His grandfather's mysterious death provided that lesson. During the American Revolution, he saw slaves joining the enemy if offered freedom. When Madison learned about slaves plotting to assist British troops, it frightened him. "It is prudent such attempts should be concealed as well as suppressed," he confided to a friend in a letter.

This is the conflict reduced to its simplest terms: James Madison, the political leader and revolutionary, knew that slavery was wrong. But Madison the slaveholder was ruled by fear and self-interest.

By 1799, when Paul Jennings was born, more than one hundred enslaved people worked at Montpelier. Most lived near the fields where they labored, far from the main house. The household servants—on call around the clock—lived close to the main house in a cluster of wooden cabins, some two stories tall and housing two or more families in tight quarters. These rough homes stood directly behind the large, elegant brick house that Madison and his family shared with his aged mother—who lived into her nineties.

The main house at Montpelier was grand, filled with classical paintings, elegant draperies, and fine carpets. Madison's books of history and philosophy crowded his library shelves. On one side of the house was a large, open second-floor balcony where Madison and his guests could sit and sip cold drinks and look out toward the mountains looming in the west. Ice cut from a pond in winter and stored beneath an open structure called the Temple chilled food and drinks in Virginia's summer heat. From the balcony, Madison and his guests also looked down at the nearby slave quarters and outbuildings, worlds apart yet completely locked together.

After Madison's return to Montpelier at the end of his presidency, many guests came to the estate. Prominent politicians made the pilgrimage to meet with the former president and Father of the Constitution, seeking his advice on the major issues confronting the nation. One of the most frequent visitors was Thomas Jefferson, who lived a few miles away. Jennings later said of the two men, "He and Mr. Madison... were extremely intimate; in fact, two brothers could not have been more so."

When Jefferson and other guests visited, formal dinners

were often held. Few subjects were discussed more around the dinner table than the future of American slavery. As Paul Jennings served food and drinks, he must have listened, perhaps wondering what their words meant for his life and his family's.

Among those famous visitors was the French hero of the American Revolution, the Marquis de Lafayette, who visited Montpelier when he toured America in 1824 and 1825. An outspoken abolitionist, Lafayette criticized his American patriot friends for failing to put an end to slavery. Lafayette had already attempted without success to convince George Washington to emancipate his slaves and allow them to live in freedom on an island Lafayette offered to purchase.

Like Jefferson, Madison hoped for an end to slavery. But, like Jefferson, he also believed that America could never be an integrated society, with whites and blacks living together under one government. In 1826, Madison wrote to Lafayette, "The two races cannot co-exist, both being free & equal."

To Madison, the only viable plan was gradual, compensated emancipation. This meant that slowly over time, the government would pay owners for their slaves, who would be freed and sent to a colony either in the American West or in Africa. Thomas Jefferson, James Monroe, and other American

*The Temple, a Roman-inspired outbuilding at Madison's Montpelier plantation.*
[Author's collection]

political leaders favored this idea, which led to the formation of the American Colonization Society in 1816.

While it might have seemed like a grand plan, the concept was fatally flawed. Two different groups opposed it for very different reasons. First, slaveholders would not abandon a system that provided their fortunes and political strength. The growing number of people in servitude—more than 1.8 million were counted in 1820—meant more seats in Congress and more electoral votes under the Constitution's three-fifths rule. In any age or country, people do not easily surrender wealth and power.

Second, the growing millions of African Americans, both freemen and those in bondage, opposed the idea. Generations of blacks had been born in America. They did not want to leave the only home they had ever known. To them, Africa was as foreign as it was to white Americans. Some free African Americans spoke out, yet the notion of colonization persisted— even Abraham Lincoln favored it as a presidential candidate in 1860. Ultimately, about 15,000 black Americans sailed back to Africa, most of them going to Liberia in West Africa, which was planned and founded as a homeland for emancipated American slaves.

Moral issues aside, the practical problem remained. Even wealthy, powerful men like Madison, Washington, and Jefferson who were considering emancipation couldn't do so without losing their fortunes. It was a simple question of dollars and cents. Their plantations and businesses would not earn enough money to support the cost of operating these large properties if they shifted to paid labor. If crops failed or prices for tobacco and wheat fell, as they often did, farmers went into debt. The only way to raise money was to sell off the two things of value they owned—land or enslaved workers, their most valuable "property."

Like George Washington and Thomas Jefferson, James Madison stated a desire not to sell any of his enslaved people. But even Founding Fathers and former presidents must pay their bills. Madison was forced to sell some of Montpelier's enslaved workers to a relative, who moved them to Louisiana. Struggling under piles of debt and in ill health, an aging Madison resolved to emancipate

*An engraving of James Madison at age eighty-two.*

"his people." He thought he would do so after his and Dolley's deaths. But he never put an actual plan in place to accomplish that.

James Madison was alive when Thomas Jefferson and John Adams both died on July 4, 1826. And he was alive when James Monroe died on July 4, 1831. As he lay sick in June 1836, doctors asked Madison if he would like medication that might help him survive until Independence Day. Madison declined.

Paul Jennings was at James Madison's bedside on June 28, 1836, the day he died. The maid Sukey had brought Madison his breakfast that morning, but he had had trouble swallowing. Madison's niece, Nelly Willis, asked her uncle, "What is the matter?"

Jennings recorded Madison's subsequent last words as "Nothing more than a change of mind, my dear."

Jennings later said that James Madison died "as quietly as the snuff of a candle goes out."

"Mr. Madison, I think, was one of the best men that ever lived," Jennings later stated. "I never saw him in a passion, and never knew him to strike a slave, although he had over one hundred; neither would he allow an overseer to do it. Whenever any slaves were reported to him as stealing or 'cutting up' badly, he would send for them and admonish them privately, and

*James Madison's grave marker at his Montpelier home.* [Author's collection]

never mortify them by doing it before others. They generally served him very faithfully."

By the time of Madison's death, thirty-seven-year-old Paul Jennings was "married" to a woman named Fanny. Together they had five children who lived with Fanny on a neighboring plantation. Paul Jennings remained Dolley Madison's property and traveled back and forth to Washington with her and a few other household servants beginning in 1837.

Moving between Washington and Montpelier meant frequent separations from Fanny and their children: Felix, William, Frances, John, and Franklin. Even when he was at Montpelier, Jennings could visit his family only once a week. It must have been heartbreaking when Jennings returned to the country estate and found his wife on her deathbed in the spring of 1844.

"Pore fanney," he wrote to Sukey, who was back at the city house. "I am looking every day to see the last of her."

Fanny Jennings died on August 4, 1844. It was the same year that Dolley Madison, facing severe financial difficulties, sold Montpelier, along with about half of its enslaved people. Dolley kept another twenty-five enslaved servants for herself and her son, Payne, a heavy drinker and gambler whose debts were a major source of Dolley's money woes.

But Paul Jennings had hopes of freedom. Jennings believed that Madison intended to free him, and he argued his case with the widowed Dolley. Although he never reported exactly what Dolley told him, Jennings knew she planned to free him after her death, as she wrote in her 1841 will, "I give to my mulatto man Paul his freedom"—the only Montpelier servant singled out for freedom after she died.

But as she lived on, harsh economic realities dashed his hopes. Struggling to make ends meet, Dolley "rented out" Jennings in 1845 to James Polk, the eleventh president and another slaveholder. According to an abolitionist newspaper that had picked up Jennings's story, Dolley kept his earnings "to the last red cent."

Returning to the White House as an enslaved servant must have been soul crushing. But when he later recounted his return to the White House, Jennings voiced no bitterness over the deferred promise of freedom.

Desperate for cash, the financially strapped Dolley accepted $200 as payment for Paul Jennings in September 1846. This sale was part of a deal Jennings had arranged with Daniel Webster, a famous senator from Massachusetts. Webster, a leading opponent of slavery, had a reputation as a friend to enslaved people. Jennings wanted help in obtaining his freedom.

In March 1847, Webster described the arrangement he had made with Jennings. "I have paid $120 for the freedom of Paul Jennings—He agrees to work out the sum, at 8 dollars a month, to be furnished with board, clothes & washing. . . . His free-dom papers I gave to him." (Through a middleman, Jennings may have worked off the $80 difference in purchase prices.)

It was well known that Webster would purchase enslaved people and allow them to work for a salary until they had repaid their purchase price. The forty-eight-year-old Paul Jennings was a free man.

Truth is sometimes stranger than fiction, and it might be easy to imagine that Paul Jennings could never forgive the way Dolley Madison had treated him. But while he worked for Senator Webster, Jennings reported that he helped out his former mistress. She had once been the nation's "Queen," admired and adored, a woman who once held Washington in her sway. But she had fallen on hard times. She came into some money only when Congress paid her a reported $25,000 in 1848 for her husband's notes on the Constitutional Convention.

"In the last days of her life, before Congress purchased her husband's papers, she was in a state of absolute poverty, and I think sometimes suffered for the necessaries of life," Jennings said. "While I was a servant to Mr. Webster, he often sent me to her with a market-basket full of provisions, and told me when-ever I saw anything in the house that I thought she was in need of, to take it to her. I often did this, and occasionally gave her small sums from my own pocket, though I had years before bought my freedom of her."

The story of Paul Jennings working off his purchase price after nearly half a century of slavery is remarkable enough. But as a free man, his life was also noteworthy. A year after he gained his freedom, Jennings is widely believed to have helped organize the largest attempted nonviolent slave escape in the United States, a plot that ultimately failed.

On April 15, 1848, seventy-seven enslaved people attempted to escape Washington by sailing on a schooner called *The Pearl*. Historian Elizabeth Dowling Taylor states, "Paul Jennings was one of the local African-American leaders who organized this scheme with Northern abolitionists."

The escape plot was foiled when winds delayed the sailing, and an enslaved man—possibly a runaway who was flogged by the men who caught him—revealed the plan to authorities.

Most of those trying to escape aboard *The Pearl* were recaptured and sold to traders who took them to the Deep South. Among them was fifteen-year-old Ellen Stewart, the daughter of Dolley Madison's longtime maid, Sukey. For a girl of her age to risk all for freedom must have been terrifying. Like Ona Judge a half century earlier, she might have acted because she feared her fate as she watched Dolley Madison sell off the remaining slaves.

Paul Jennings may have hidden Ellen Stewart and then helped her get aboard *The Pearl*. After she was recaptured, Ellen was sold to slave traders but was later repurchased by abolitionists and taken north. By 1848, Dolley Madison had sold Sukey; Sukey's fate after the sale is unclear. Through their years together, Dolley had often written about Sukey's faults, but she had kept her all that time. In the end, she was just too desperate for money to hold on to Sukey. Dolley Madison died in July 1849.

*The Pearl* incident provoked a riot in Washington when the ship and escapees were brought back to the city. A proslavery mob attacked an abolitionist newspaper and other known antislavery activists. These events prompted a slavery debate in Congress—and may have influenced one piece of the Compromise of 1850, which ended the slave trade in the District of Columbia.

But a question remains: How did Paul Jennings come to play a role in *The Pearl* escape?

The answer to that question has never been clear. It was never made public in his lifetime. While Jennings was by then a free man, there were still strict laws in Washington called Black Codes. Left over from earlier times, these harsh rules limited how late black people could be on the street at night or how many of them could gather, even for social visits. The codes also limited the freedoms and opportunities of free African Americans—for instance, only certain jobs, such as driving a cart, were open to blacks.

There is little doubt that if Jennings had been tried and

convicted of involvement in *The Pearl* incident, his punishment would have been severe. Two of the white men involved were imprisoned for four years before being pardoned by President Millard Fillmore.

But a family of people who were later freed said, "None did more valiant service, both by advice and actual soliciting for funds than their true friend and sympathizer, Paul Jennings."

While Paul Jennings escaped notice in this controversy, he achieved real fame for another reason. After he won his freedom, he secured a job in the Pension Office, with the recommendation of Senator Webster. Part of the Interior Department, the office handled the business of pensions paid to former government employees, including veterans. With an annual salary of $400, Jennings was paid less than white workers. But he was able to save enough money to acquire a house and property in Washington's black neighborhood. He married Desdemona Brooks in 1849, and by 1854, Jennings had bought a lot in the capital city on the south side of L Street, between 18th and 19th Streets. Jennings resided at 1804 L Street, while his daughter, Frances, and her two sons lived next door, where he later purchased a second home.

While at the Pension Office, Jennings met a man named John Brooks Russell, a black freeman from Massachusetts. As the two men talked, Jennings revealed more about his life with the Madisons. Fascinated by the stories he heard, Russell encouraged Jennings to allow him to write down these recollections—of life in Washington, Jennings's role in the events of 1814, and his long relationship with James and Dolley Madison.

In 1863, an article entitled "A Colored Man's Reminiscences of James Madison" appeared in a historical magazine. Its preface, written by J.B.R. (John Brooks Russell), spoke of Jennings: "His character for sobriety, truth, and fidelity, is unquestioned; and as he was a daily witness of interesting events, I have thought some of his recollections were worth writing down in almost his own language."

*A Colored Man's Reminiscences of James Madison* was later published in book form. Considered the first memoir of anyone, black or white, who ever served in the White House, the book appeared in 1865, the same year that the Civil War ended and the Thirteenth Amendment, abolishing slavery forever in America, was added to the U.S. Constitution.

After Abraham Lincoln issued the Emancipation Proclamation in January 1863, black men were permitted to enlist in the Union army. Paul Jennings was in his sixties during the Civil War—too old to fight. But many other African Americans rose to the challenge, and by the end of the war, black men counted for about 10 percent of Union forces. These included the sons of Paul Jennings. Born enslaved, John, Franklin, and William

Jennings all enlisted and served. Franklin Jennings was with the Fifth Massachusetts Colored Volunteer Cavalry, which was given the honor of entering Richmond, the fallen Confederate capital, on April 3, 1865.

A few weeks later, Paul Jennings most likely would have joined the thousands of African Americans who turned out in the streets for the funeral procession of Abraham Lincoln, who died on April 15, assassinated by John Wilkes Booth.

In 1870, at the age of seventy-one, after the earlier death of his second wife, Desdemona, he married a third woman, Amelia Dorsey. Paul Jennings died at his home on L Street on May 20, 1874.

Although Paul Jennings was buried in a Washington cemetery, his remains were later removed, and their ultimate resting place is unknown.

# SLAVERY IN AMERICA TIME LINE
## 1829–1838

**1829**
- President Andrew Jackson offers to buy Texas from Mexico; the offer is rejected. In August, Mexico outlaws slavery but allows Texans to keep their slaves. The following year, Mexico forbids further American colonization of Texas and prohibits the importation of more slaves into the territory.
- Georgia passes a law that prohibits the education of slaves or free blacks. Other Southern states soon follow.
- David Walker, a free black man born in Wilmington, North Carolina, publishes *Appeal to the Coloured Citizens of the World*, an angry denunciation of slavery that calls on enslaved people to rise up and cast off their chains.

**1830**
The U.S. population is counted as 12,866,020; a total of 2,328,767 black people live in the United States. Of those, 2,009,050 are enslaved people.

**1831**
- Abolitionist William Lloyd Garrison begins publication of his militant antislavery journal, *The Liberator*.
- One of the most violent slave uprisings in American history, the Nat Turner Rebellion, takes place in Southampton County, Virginia. About forty men join leader Nat Turner, whose owner is killed along with at least fifty-four other white people in the deadly rebellion. Turner is captured and executed. Following this revolt by slaves, abolitionist writings are censored and harsher slave codes are passed.

**1832**
- The New England Anti-Slavery Society (later known as the Massachusetts Anti-Slavery Society) is organized at the African Baptist Church in Boston. Later that year, the first female abolitionist group, the Female Anti-Slavery Society of Salem, forms in Massachusetts.
- Andrew Jackson is reelected president.

**1833**
- Great Britain outlaws slavery in all its colonies, freeing 700,000 people from enslavement. Their owners are compensated.
- In Philadelphia, the Female Anti-Slavery Society is founded by, among others, Charlotte Forten, granddaughter of black abolition pioneer James Forten, and Lucretia Mott and Elizabeth Cady Stanton, two future leaders of the women's rights movement.

**1836**
- Petitions asking to outlaw slavery in Washington, D.C., are presented to Congress. In May, Congress adopts a gag rule designed to prohibit any discussion of petitions related to slavery.
- Arkansas, a slave state, becomes the twenty-fifth state.
- Martin Van Buren of New York is elected the eighth U.S. president. He is sympathetic to the slaveholding South and opposes any limit on slavery.

**1837**
- Michigan becomes the twenty-sixth state, a free state.
- Abolitionist publisher Elijah Lovejoy is killed by a proslavery mob in Alton, Illinois.

**1838**
- In May, Pennsylvania Hall is destroyed by fire after it hosts an antislavery meeting.
- The Underground Railroad, a system of safe houses used to assist enslaved people escaping to the North, is organized. One of its leaders is Robert Purvis, a wealthy mixed-race abolitionist who had inherited a large amount of money from his white father, a cotton broker.

## CHAPTER SEVEN

# "HOW WOULD YOU LIKE TO BE A SLAVE?"

# THE STORY OF ALFRED JACKSON

Stop the Runaway. Fifty Dollars Reward. . . .
A Mulatto Man Slave, about thirty years old, six feet
and an inch high, stout made and active, talks sensible,
stoops in his walk, and has a remarkable large foot . . .
will pass for a free man. . . . The above reward will be
given any person that will take him . . . and ten dollars
extra, for every hundred lashes any person will give
him, to the amount of three hundred.
—ANDREW JACKSON, ADVERTISING FOR THE RETURN OF A
RUNAWAY SLAVE IN THE *TENNESSEE GAZETTE AND METRO
DISTRICT ADVERTISER*, SEPTEMBER 26, 1804

You white folks have easy times, don't you?
—ALFRED JACKSON

*Born enslaved in 1802 at Andrew Jackson's Hermitage plantation, Alfred Jackson
spent his entire life on the property, until his death in 1901.* [Andrew Jackson's
Hermitage]

211

t was Christmas 1838. For the enslaved people of the Hermitage, Andrew Jackson's Tennessee plantation, that meant a holiday. For most enslaved Americans, it was their only holiday.

"We didn't know but one holiday, that was Christmas day," Baily Cunningham, born enslaved in Virginia, recalled many years later. "And it was not much different from any other day. The field hands did not have to work on Christmas day. We didn't have any Christmas presents."

This December night would be different. A large group of people, perhaps forty to as many as a hundred, from Jackson's Hermitage plantation and several nearby farms had gathered for a celebration. It was not going to be an evening of joyous caroling and exchanging gifts around a Christmas tree. It was to be a lively party with music, dancing, and drinking.

At some point during the festivities, Alfred, one of the enslaved men from the Hermitage, "cryed out he was the best man in the House and [an] altercation ensued," said a woman at the party. According to an account of a later trial, she said, "Alfred and cancer [another man present] got afighting, and George and Walis got in contact."

Possibly started by an argument over one man's boast, a fistfight followed. Soon it moved outdoors and turned into a

The Christmas Week, *an 1863 illustration by Henry Louis Stephens, depicts* African Americans celebrating Christmas. [Library of Congress, Prints & Photographs Division, LC-USZC4-2527]

riotous brawl, most likely fueled by alcohol. As others joined the fray, one man named Frank attempted to stop the fight. Then several other men attacked him.

"Frank picked up a bench or plank and retreated back," according to a later courtroom account recorded by Andrew Jackson. She testified she saw "Alfred strike Frank with a rock in the breast, Frank bent forward, when Jack struck him on the head with a rock and dashed his brains out." She also said that she "heard the scull break." Another witness said that both Alfred and Frank had picked up rocks.

No matter who struck the blow, Frank lay dead.

Legally, Frank was the property of Stockley Donelson, a relative and neighbor of President Andrew Jackson. Donelson demanded that four men from Jackson's property be arrested for murder. For an enslaved man in Tennessee at that time, a murder conviction would have resulted in a swift death sentence.

For his part, Andrew Jackson was convinced that the men from the Hermitage were innocent. He did not want enslaved men from his property to be singled out. So many others had been involved in this riot that Jackson thought it was impossible to say who was responsible.

At the time, Andrew Jackson was no ordinary man. He was the most powerful and popular man in America following two terms in the White House. A wartime general and president beloved by many Americans as Old Hickory and the Hero of

New Orleans, he was second in stature only to George Washington as the nation's most admired leader.

But none of that mattered. In spite of Jackson's prestige and his protests, a warrant was issued for George, Alfred, Jack, and Squire, another man involved in the fight. All four were members of the Hermitage plantation's large enslaved "family," as Jackson called them. The four men were arrested and held in a Nashville jail to await trial.

Freedom came swiftly for one. A grand jury cleared George of wrongdoing. Born enslaved around 1800, George was the son of a cook in the Jackson household named Hannah. He had been Jackson's longtime body servant, just as Billy Lee and Paul Jennings had been beside George Washington and James Madison. George had been with Jackson during two terms at the White House, and he would later stand at Jackson's deathbed.

While George was released, the other three men would be tried. Jack, listed as a field laborer, was married to Aggy, the daughter of Jackson's trusted carriage driver, Charles, and Charlotte, a house servant. Squire was George's brother. A foreman, he ran the Hermitage cotton gin—an important position on the farm, where cotton was a cash crop.

The last of these men was Alfred, the nephew of George and Squire. Alfred was the son of Ned, an enslaved carpenter, and Betty, a cook and maid. Betty had given birth to Alfred in 1802. As the child of a house servant, Alfred would have begun working as a young boy doing household chores like fetching water and firewood.

There are many accounts of what fieldwork and household duties were like for enslaved adults. It is rarer to glimpse the way enslaved children like Alfred were put to work. One hint is found in a book published in 1915 describing Hermitage life. According to the author, "One of these same dusky pickaninnies was employed to wield the fanciful fly brush, made of peacock feathers, while the family were at meals."

Now considered an offensive term, *pickaninny* was once a common word used to describe young enslaved children who often carried wood and water and did other simple household chores, like swatting flies from the dinner table. The term may come from the Spanish words *pequeño* (for small) and *niño* (for child). The author of that 1915 book also wrote, "Those old plantation days were not so bad," reflecting white views of enslaved life that lasted for decades.

As a young man, Alfred's tasks changed. He became an expert with Jackson's horses, driving carriages and wagons, and was much admired for his handling of Jackson's prized stable. He also rode Jackson's horses in races, and visitors to the Hermitage were struck by how tall and powerful he was. His favorite team of horses was Dicey and Sugar Stick, and "when he was driving the carriage, the ladies always felt safe."

\* \* \*

Losing Alfred, Jack, and Squire would count as a devastating blow to Andrew Jackson. Age seventy-one and in poor health, he had been through a lifetime of war, brawls, political battles, and eight often stormy years as president. He had even survived an assassination attempt.

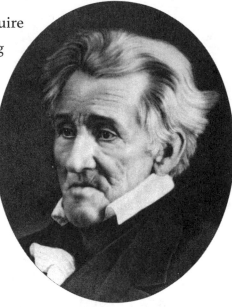

On top of his other troubles, Jackson had serious money problems. He faced high expenses and a poor

*Photographer Mathew Brady captured this image of former president Andrew Jackson in 1845, months before his death at age seventy-eight.*

economy. Rich in land and slaves, he was cash poor. As prices for cotton dropped, Andrew Jackson fell deeper into debt.

Still, Andrew Jackson hired three of Nashville's most prominent attorneys to defend the men. The bill for that defense came in at $1,500—a significant amount of money at that time. But Jackson stood by Alfred and the others. To cover the cost, Jackson had to borrow cash and sell off some land.

The former president attended every day of the trial, which began in Nashville in January 1839. Jackson took notes of the testimony. He did not testify, but his mere presence spoke for

*The main house at the Hermitage as depicted in the 1850s, a few years after Andrew Jackson's death. The tomb of Andrew and Rachel Jackson is within the small domed structure seen in the center background, which is located in the formal garden beside the main house.* [Library of Congress, Prints & Photographs Division, LC-DIG-ppmsca-23683]

him. Perhaps the sight of the aging, much-admired war hero and president helped sway the jury. When the trial was over, all three men were found not guilty and released to return to the Hermitage.

The tale of the 1838 Christmas riot is special, and not simply because a former president stood by some enslaved men. The story of Alfred Jackson and the others at that holiday gathering offers a very different look at the lives of enslaved people. Slavery is often depicted only in terms of the work that was done for masters. But enslaved people had a world of their own. This is the human side of the story that schoolbooks and histories often overlook. In what little free time they had, they fished and hunted, quilted and kept chickens, tended their gardens, and had children who played with simple toys such as marbles or animals roughly carved from wood.

On Sundays, most enslaved people went to church. That was also the day when men traveled to other plantations where they had "away" families. At night, the slave quarters came to life with singing and dancing, storytelling, and prayer meetings. While Christianity had become a central part of

*A nineteenth-century toy marble found at a Hermitage excavation.* [Andrew Jackson's Hermitage]

the enslaved people's world, African religious traditions still carried on. And, as happened at the Christmas party, enslaved people sometimes fought, committed crimes, and had rivalries and disputes in the societies they created.

Of course, those enslaved societies were ruled by the will or whims of white masters. There can be no mistake: masters were in control. Many slaveholders could be cruel, fickle, and unforgiving. Harsh punishment for the slightest offense was never far away—even from so-called humane slave owners. But enslaved men and women met, fell in love, had families— sometimes on a farm or plantation other than their own—and went dancing at parties. It is important to emphasize this because the word *slave* itself defines these people in such a narrow way.

Small tastes of freedom, joy, and celebration were permitted, or even encouraged, because from the master's point of view, it made sense to allow a measure of comfort and happiness. Many slaveholders believed that happy and contented enslaved workers—at least from the master's perspective—made better workers. So they tolerated some limited, basic human pleasures. Just as important, many of them thought that a man with family ties was much less likely to attempt escape.

But a puzzling question remains: Why would Andrew Jackson go to such great personal expense and spend his days at the trial of some enslaved men? After all, there were about 150 enslaved people at the Hermitage by this time—placing Andrew Jackson among the largest slaveholders in the state of Tennessee.

There is no simple answer. Andrew Jackson was not an all-around nice guy who was sympathetic and humane to the enslaved people who worked for him. He did not hesitate to use the whip, as he once suggested in an 1804 advertisement that called for as many as three hundred lashes—a near death sentence. He instructed his overseers to use a cowhide to whip or beat servants who were rude or misbehaved in some way. Certainly it was a question of dollars and cents. These enslaved men had great value on the trading blocks. Losing them probably would have cost more than what Jackson spent on their defense.

But was it more than simple accounting? In the thorny and sometimes confusing world of America's masters and enslaved people, did Andrew Jackson have any affection for these men? Did he look at these "hands"—as he would have called them—as family members? Or was it his macho nature not to lose a fight?

It is hard to say what Jackson felt about this question. Unlike Jefferson and Madison, who both wrote and spoke at length about slavery and their feelings about some of their enslaved people, Andrew Jackson made few comments on the subject. In letters to people who ran the farm while he was in the White House, he discussed the treatment of enslaved people along

with cotton prices, which crops to plant, and other day-to-day affairs at the Hermitage. But Jackson displayed no sign of a conscience bothered by slavery because it was evil. To him, slavery, in all its harsh brutality, was a fact of life.

The accounts of some of the Hermitage's enslaved workers hint at the affectionate feelings shared by owner and enslaved. A formerly enslaved woman later spoke of Andrew Jackson as a "kind master" in an 1880 interview, long after Jackson's death. She told how as a small girl she would comb "ole master's hair" and pick out "buggers." When he once caught young Hannah in a fib, she recalled, Jackson said, " 'I knew you was telling a story. But never mind. I am going to buy you a new dress if you promise me you will never tell another.' I promised and he bought me the dress. I remember it was red. I don't believe I ever did tell him a story after that."

Were these honest recollections? Or just words to please a white person?

Andrew Jackson expressed no desire to see an end to slavery, as Washington, Jefferson, and Madison had. Even as he spoke passionately about freedom and his rights, he never thought these ideals applied to black people in chains. A fierce defender of individual liberty, he would have included the

The Lash, *an illustrated postcard from 1863 by artist Henry Louis Stephens, depicts a lashing.* [Library of Congress, Prints & Photographs Division, LC-USZ62-41839]

power to own slaves as one of those basic rights. And he had
the Constitution to back him up.

Unlike his predecessors Washington, Jefferson, Madison, and
Monroe, Andrew Jackson was born far from Virginia's privileged world of well-to-do planters. And he wasn't raised in the
more refined world of Boston, like John Adams and John
Quincy Adams, two other men who had preceded him as president. He had never traveled to Europe's royal courts.

Andrew Jackson was the first "rags to riches" president.
Born on March 15, 1767, in a rugged cabin near Waxhaw Creek,
a border area between North and South Carolina, he grew up
in a rough-and-tumble frontier of hardship and war. It was a
realm of basic "eye for an eye" justice. His parents were Scots-
Irish immigrants who had arrived in America two years earlier. Just weeks before Andrew Jackson was born, his father
died. Jackson's mother, with three young mouths to feed,
earned a living tending eight children of nearby relatives.

During the American Revolution, Andrew Jackson's oldest
brother, Hugh, was killed while fighting the British in 1779. As
teenagers, Andrew and his other brother, Robert, then joined
their uncle's militia company as couriers carrying messages
and news of battles. In the savage fighting in South Carolina,
the British hunted down rebel fighters, and the Jackson boys
and a cousin were captured in April 1781.

In a story made popular after the war, a British officer ordered young Andrew Jackson to clean the officer's muddy boots, which the boy refused to do. The officer struck the young boy with a saber, leaving a gash on his hand and head. But young Andrew still refused the order. This story, embellished or not, became part of Andrew Jackson's legacy as a defiant and lifelong enemy of the British and the world of privilege and aristocracy they represented.

The Brave Boy of Waxhaws *is an 1876 Currier & Ives lithograph depicting an incident in Andrew Jackson's childhood in which he supposedly stood up to a British officer.* [Library of Congress, Prints & Photographs Division, LC-USZ62-2340]

All three boys were taken to a crowded, filthy prison camp, where smallpox raged through the inmates. Andrew's mother somehow persuaded the British to release the boys. They returned home, but two days later Andrew's brother, Robert, died of smallpox. In November 1781, Jackson's mother also died after nursing victims of a wartime cholera epidemic on a ship in Charleston, South Carolina.

His family wiped out by disease and war, fourteen-year-old orphan Andrew Jackson first lived with relatives and later moved to North Carolina. One man who knew Jackson there said he was "the most roaring, rollicking, game-cocking, card-playing, mischievous fellow, that ever lived in Salisbury."

The riotous youngster eventually settled down and became an attorney. Moving to the newly opened and somewhat lawless territory that would become Tennessee, he bartered his services as a Nashville lawyer in return for land and enslaved people, trading for a woman named Nancy in 1788. Besides the practical value of someone to cook and clean, owning servants was a status symbol an ambitious young attorney needed to impress neighbors and legal clients.

For a time, Jackson lived in the boardinghouse of Mrs. John Donelson and her dark-haired, pipe-smoking daughter, Rachel. At the time, Rachel was married to a man named Robards but was living apart from him. While waiting for a divorce—a very rare thing in those days—Rachel Robards fell in love with

Andrew Jackson. They were married in August 1791. But trouble was brewing. Rachel's divorce had not been legally granted at the time of their wedding, so Rachel Robards was still married to her first husband when she married Andrew Jackson, a crime known as bigamy. After the divorce was granted, they were married a second time, on January 7, 1794. That remedy came back to haunt the Jacksons.

As Jackson's land holdings, fame, and political ambitions grew, so did nasty gossip about Rachel's first marriage. The hot-tempered Jackson responded violently to any insult about his wife. To defend her honor, Jackson shot and killed a Nashville attorney in a duel in 1806.

With the War of 1812, Andrew Jackson became a larger-than-life American idol. Commanding Tennessee militiamen, he refused to leave any of his sick or wounded men behind after a long march, earning the admiring nickname Old Hickory. His men said Jackson was as tall and tough as an iron-hard hickory tree.

His reputation as a fierce soldier began during a hard-fought war against the Creeks, a native nation allied with the British. After months of brutal fighting marked by massacres and ruthless combat, Jackson pushed the Creek nation out of its ancestral lands. The Creeks were brought to their knees and forced to turn over some twenty million acres of territory to the United States. After one ferocious battle in which Jackson's men cut off the noses of dead Creeks to tally the casualties, the Indians also gave Jackson a nickname—Sharp Knife.

Nowadays, many people assume that most of the fighting between the American government and American Indians took place on the Great Plains and in the Southwest in the late nineteenth century. Hollywood Westerns focused on that story. But in fact, the fighting started when Europeans first arrived, and it continued for centuries. Andrew Jackson's battles with the Creeks were part of a long string of wars fought for decades against tribes of the American Southeast, including the Cherokee, Chickasaw, Choctaw, and Seminoles. Often known as the Five Civilized Tribes, all would eventually be wiped out or forcibly removed from their lands, some on the infamous Trail of Tears in 1831.

Jackson's fame was cemented with his greatest wartime victory in January 1815. Patching together an odd assortment of regular soldiers, local militiamen, pirates, black freemen, and enslaved men, he defeated a large and more experienced British army at the Battle of New Orleans with very few losses.

His legend growing, Jackson heard that an aging Thomas Jefferson had offered a toast in honor of his victory. But Old Hickory was unimpressed. The battle-hardened Jackson

*Jackson led troops at the Battle of Horseshoe Bend (Tohopeka) during the Creek War in 1814, in present-day southern Alabama.* [Art and Picture Collection, The New York Public Library, b17168662]

had no respect for Jefferson, the man who had fled from Richmond and Monticello when chased by redcoats during the Revolution—the events described in Isaac Granger's story (see Chapter Five). "I am glad the old gentleman has plucked up courage enough to at least attend a banquet in honor of a battle," Jackson said sarcastically.

Jackson had little more respect for the enslaved men who had stood beside him at New Orleans. They had been promised liberation, but as historian Gene Allen Smith wrote, "Once Jackson had secured victory, he denied slaves their promised freedom while he had white armed troops to enforce his decision."

*John Quincy Adams, sixth president of the United States and son of the second president, John Adams. His victory in the election of 1824 enraged Jackson and his followers and began a bitter feud between the two men.* [Bureau of Engraving and Printing]

With his popularity soaring after the War of 1812, Jackson ran for president in 1824, hoping to succeed President James Monroe. While Jackson won the popular vote, none of the five candidates in the running that year received enough electoral votes to win. Instead, the election was decided in the House of Representatives, which voted John Quincy Adams the nation's sixth president.

Believing he was cheated out of the presidency, Jackson immediately began to campaign against Adams and easily defeated him in 1828 in one of the nastiest presidential races ever. One piece of the mudslinging was the Coffin Handbill, a famous campaign poster published by Adams supporters that showed rows of coffins and listed Jackson's "bloody deeds"— his duels, the deaths of militiamen under his command.

Andrew Jackson's wife, Rachel, was not spared from cruel campaign gossip. Supporters of Adams said that Rachel Jackson was guilty of adultery and bigamy. These personal attacks devastated Rachel Jackson, and she soon became seriously ill. In December 1828, Rachel Jackson died from an apparent heart attack while reluctantly preparing to move to the White House. Attired in the white dress she had planned to wear to his inauguration, Jackson's beloved wife was buried on Christmas Eve in the garden at the Hermitage.

At Rachel's burial, Jackson angrily said, "I can and do forgive all my enemies. But those vile wretches who have slandered her must look to God for mercy." A bitter Jackson set off for the White House, believing that the vicious attacks on his wife had caused her death and vowing revenge on his political opponents. When he arrived in Washington in March 1829,

## SUPPLEMENT TO THE DEMOCRATIC PRESS, GIVING A BRIEF ACCOUNT OF SOME OF THE BLOODY DEEDS OF

# General Jackson.

JACOB WEBB.
DAVID MORROW.
JOHN HARRIS.
HENRY LEWIS.
DAVID HUNT.
EDWARD LINDSEY.

Every Reader probably knows that the names over the above coffins were the names of *Six Militia Men*, who entered into their country's service in the late war, as they believed, as they were told by their officers, and as the law declared, *for three* months. At the end of that time they drew their rations, gave up their guns, took receipts for them, and returned to their families. A dispute arose; it was said they ought to have served *six* months; Gen. Jackson directed them, and several hundred other Militia men, who had also returned home, to be pursued and brought back to camp. Some returned, and some were brought back. General Jackson ordered a Court Martial, and the unhappy men whose names are over the above Coffins were found Guilty, and sentenced to suffer death. The proceedings of the court, which were in many respects irregular, were forwarded to General Jackson, who instead of forwarding them to the President, approved himself of their sentences, and issued a general order, directing that these six Militia-Men should, in defiance of Law, and of every dictate of Humanity, be SHOT TO DEATH, within four days. How they were shot is detailed in the following narrative, which was written by one who was present at the dreadful scene, and saw the melancholy sight he describes. His account was published in the *Democratic Press* of February 2, 1828, which is more than seven months ago. The time of the publication is specially mentioned, because it will be seen, in the account, that the EYE WITNESS to this scene of Blood and Carnage, appealed to Col. Russell, *the commanding officer, on the day the six Militia Men were shot*, "for the *truth* of every word he relates." From that day to this, although Col. Russell is a Jackson man, and notwithstanding all the pains that have been taken in the last seven months, Col. Russell never has been prevailed upon to contradict one word of the following faithful narrative.

### *A Brief Account of the Execution of the Six Militia Men.*

As we may soon expect to have the *official* documents in relation to the Six Militia Men, arrested, tried, and put to death, under the orders of General Andrew Jackson, this may not be an improper time to give to the public some of the particulars of their execution, as we have them from "An Eye Witness," who appeals to Col. Russell, for the truth of every word he relates.

Harris was a Baptist Preacher, with a large family. He had hired, as a substitute, for three months. This was the case with most of them. They were ignoront men, but obstinate in what they believed right, and what they had been told by their officers was right. They were all sure they could not be kept beyond three months; they gave up their musquets, and had provisions dealt out to them, from the public stores, before they left the camp. This confirmed their convictions that they were right, and doing that which was lawful.

Col. Russell commanded at the execution. The Militia men were brought to the place in a large wagon. The military dispositions being made, Col. Russell rode up to the wagon and ordered the men to descend. Harris was the only one who betrayed feminine weakness. The awfulness of the occasion; his wife and *nine* children; the parting with his son; and the fear of a quickly approaching ignominious death! quite overcame him, and he sunk in unmanly grief. No feeling of military pride could brace him up.

Col. Russell, doubtless, felt as a man; but he felt also for the pride of the army, and desired to animate the men with fortitude. "You are about to die," said he, "by the sentence of a Court Martial—die like men; *like soldiers*. You have been brave in the field—you have fought well—do no discredit to your country, or dishonor to the army, or yourselves, by any unmanly fears. Meet your fate with courage."

Harris attempted to make some apology for his conduct, but while he spoke, he wept bitterly. The fear of death, the idea that he should never again behold his wife and little ones, and his son weeping near him, had taken such entire possession of his mind that it was impossible he should rally.

Lewis, the gallant Lewis, said in a clear and manly tone, "Colonel, I have served my country well. I love it dearly, and would, if I could, serve it longer and better. I have fought bravely—*you know* I have, and HERE I have a right to say so, MYSELF. I would not wish to die, in this way"—here his voice faultered, and he passed the back of his right hand over his eyes—"I *did not* expect it: But, I am now as firm as I have been in battle, and [illegible] that I will die as becomes a soldier—you know I am a brave [illegible]" Other sentences were uttered, other declarations were made, and words of comfort spoken, but they were lost on me; my attention, says an Eye Witness, being chiefly directed to Lewis.

Six coffins were ranged as directed, and on each of them knelt one of our condemned American Militia Men. Such a sight was never seen before! I trust in God it never will be seen again! Six soldiers were detailed and drawn up to fire at each man. What an awful duty! Their white caps were drawn over the faces of the unhappy men. Harris evidently trembled, and I could almost persuade myself that the heart of Lewis was enlarged, and that his bosom rose with manly courage to meet death. The fatal word was given and they all fell.

As we approached the scene of blood and carnage, Lewis gave signs of life; the rest were all dead—he crawled up on his coffin. After the lapse of a few minnes, he said—I give his very words: "Colonel"—the Colonel was close to him—"Colonel, I am not killed, but I am sadly cut and mangled." His body was now examined, and it was found that four balls had wounded him. "Colonel, said he, "did I behave well?" "Yes, Lewis"—said the Colonel, in the kindest tone of voice—"like a man." "Well sir," said he, "have I not atoned for this offence? *Shall I not live?*" The Colonel was much agitated, and gave orders that the Surgeons should, if possible, preserve his life. They did all that skill and humanity could do—it was of no avail. Poor Lewis expressed a great desire to live—"not," said he at one time, "that I fear death, but I would repent me of some sins, and I desire to live yet a little longer in the world." He suffered inconceivable agony, from his wounds, and died on the fourth day.

Many a soldier has wept over his grave. He was a brave man and much beloved. He suffered twenty deaths. I have seen the big drops chase each other down his forehead with pain and anguish. There was much sensibility and sympathy throughout the camp. I would not have, unjustly and unnecessarily, signed his death warrant for all the wealth of all the Indies. The soldiers detailed to shoot Lewis had, from strong feelings of sympathy, and mistaken humanity, failed to shoot him—but four balls had entered his body. "An Eye Witness" appeals to Col. Russell, who he thinks now lives in Alabama, for the perfect truth of this sketch. He does not fear but the Colonel will keenly recollect and faithfully depict the horrors of the day on which six Americans were shot to death under his command—but not by his orders.

The order bears date the very day after *General Jackson* returned in triumph to New-Orleans, and the day before he joyfully went, under triumphal arches, to the Temple of the living God; where, says the historian, "they *crowned* their *adored* General with laurels." The order for the execution of these six unhappy men bears date January 22, 1815. His crown of laurels had not yet withered, when blood, the life's blood of his countrymen, of his fellow soldiers, flowed plentifully by his order. May that order and its consequences, sink deep into the hearts of the American people, and steel them against him who had no flesh in his obdurate heart; who did not feel for Man; who in the midst of Joy and Revelry, almost in the more immediate presence of his Creator, issued the fatal order to put his fellow creatures to death, and to make their wives and children, widows and orphans.

A short time before the execution of the six militia men, seven regular soldiers were shot to death near Nashville, by a band of regulars scarcely sufficient to guard the prisoners. They were confined in a house, and taken out and executed one at a time, there being scarcely enough of men for the purpose of executing and guarding at the same moment. An eighth soldier was to have been executed at the same time. He was a young man, who had deserted one month before his time had expired. General Jackson doomed him to die with the others. He was saved by a writ of habeas corpus from Judge M'Nairy, who fell under Jackson's displeasure for snatching this victim from his blood-stained hands. If Jackson's army had been at hand, no doubt M'Nairy would have shared the fate of Judge Hall and Judge Fromentin, and been put to prison. Capital punishments in an army are designed for example as well as for penalty; but in this case it was a transaction of horror to peaceful citizens; no army was there to witness the bloody tragedy. He has ever been a man of "blood and carnage."

Poor JOHN WOODS, he was a generous hearted, noble fellow as ever lived, who had volunteered in the service of his country. He was on guard one day at Fort Strother—the officer of the guard had permitted him to go to his tent, and snatch a hasty breakfast; whilst disposing of his scanty meal, seated on the ground beside his skillet, an upstart little officer, who was not Woods' equal at home, ordered him to pick up and carry off some bones that lay scattered about the place—Woods refused, and the little officer attempted to compel him. At this instant, General Jackson having heard the dispute, came out of his tent, and without knowing any thing of the merits of the case, repeatedly vociferated—"*Shoot the damn'd rascal!—Shoot the damn'd rascal!*" For this offence, the unfortunate, the galland Woods, was tried, condemned, and shot. Before his trial, Gen. Jackson used this language to the court martial. "*By the immortal God! if you find him guilty I will not pardon him!*" And he kept his promise; though he did offer a pardon provided he would enlist in the regular service. Thus perished as noble a fellow as ever lived, for as trifling an offence as ever took the life of man!!!

Do not be startled, gentle reader, at the picture before you. It is a true picture, and every body ought to know it. Gen. Jackson having made an assault upon Samuel Jackson, in the streets of Nashville, the latter not being disposed to stand still and be beaten, stooped down for a stone to defend himself. While in the act of stooping, Gen. Jackson drew the sword from his cane, and ran it through Samuel Jackson's body, the sword entering his back and coming out at his breast. For this offence an indictment was found against Gen. Jackson, by a grand jury, upon which he was arraigned and tried. But finding means to persuade the petit jury that he committed the act in self-defence, he was acquitted. Gentle reader, it is for you to say, whether this man, who carries a sword cane, and is willing to run it through the body of any one who may presume to stand in his way, is a fit person to be our President—to be the ruler of a peace loving People!!!

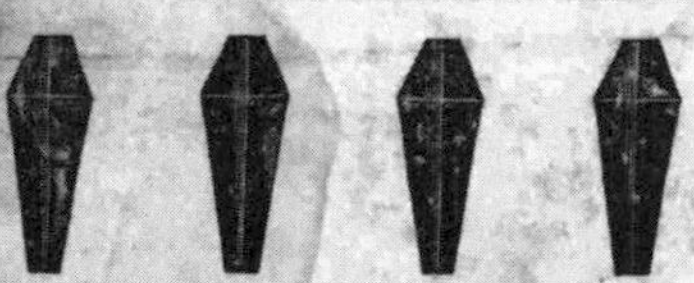

General Jackson, detailing his progress among the Indians, in the course of which, men, WOMEN and CHILDREN, were indiscriminately "exterminated," their towns burnt, and their country laid waste; with the utmost complacency and *sang froid*, says, in his letter dated, "Camp before St. Marks, April 9, 1818"—"Capt. M'Ever having hoisted English colours on board of his boats, Francis *the Prophet*, Hocomochematcho and *two others*, were *decoyed* on board. *These have been hung to-day!*" Reader, mark the perfect indifference with which Gen. Jackson shoots, hangs or stabs his fellow beings, with or without trial, and the more than callous, aye, even exulting composure, with which he details his horrid and bloody deeds! If the Indians, according to the customs of their nation, put to death a prisoner, all the feelings of our nature rise in indignation against them. With what feelings then should we contemplate the *decoying* and the cold-blooded murder of prisoners, by a civilized man, in the face of the laws and the customs of his country!

On the 27th of March, 1814, General Jackson had found at an Indian village, at the bend of the Tallapousie, about 1000 Indians, with their *squaws* and *children*, "running about among their huts!" The following is an account of the sanguinary massacre which took place:—it is Gen. Jackson's own, and therefore must be received as sufficient evidence against himself. He says:—"DETERMINING TO EXTERMINATE them, I detached Gen. Coffee with the mounted men, and nearly the whole of the Indian force, early on the morning of yesterday, to cross the river about two miles below the encampment, and surround the bend in such a manner that none of them should escape by attempting to cross the river." The result he then details:—"*Five hundred and fifty-seven were left dead on the Peninsula, and a great number of them were killed by the horsemen in attempting to cross the river*; IT IS BELIEVED THAT NO MORE THAN TEN ESCAPED. We CONTINUED to DESTROY *many of them who had concealed themselves under the banks of the river, until we were prevented by the night.* THIS MORNING WE KILLED SIXTEEN WHICH HAD BEEN CONCEALED."

We ask you to pause and reflect that the above tragic narration of cold-blooded and merciless cruelty, is taken from an official communication *made by General Andrew Jackson.*

The General, after sleeping (with what composure, we cannot say,) through the night ensuing the tragedy we speak of, awoke in the morning surrounded by the corpses of "five hundred and seventy" fellow creatures, to cause, by way of worthy afterpiece, sixteen others to be dragged from their concealments, and put to death in cold blood. We cannot boast of more than common sensibility, but we must think that to witness such an act, would make ours a little cold also. What are the General's words?—these—"this morning we killed sixteen which had been concealed"—and the man who acts and speaks thus; who has half as much blood upon his conscience, as he has upon his hands,—he, forsooth, is to be called the peer and *like* of Washington, the happy warrior,—

——————"he
Whom every man at arms could wish to be!"

But it is time to have done with the unpleasant subject. We will observe in addition to the details already given, that the village was burnt, and several women and children killed. In conclusion, we ask our fellow citizens, whether General Jackson, though he has contributed largely to the military reputation of our country, has not done enough to disqualify him, in the eyes of the people, as virtuous as they are free, for the office he seeks at their hands.

the seventh president was described as "a tall gaunt man, standing straight as a ram-rod, his face wrinkled with pain and age, his thick gray hair ... turning snow-white."

Without Rachel to man-age the household ser-vants as she had always done, one of Jackson's first challenges was to move into a White House that had been run by a paid staff

*Rachel Donelson Jackson, wife of President Andrew Jackson.* [Tennessee Portrait Project]

under John Quincy Adams and First Lady Louisa Adams. Like his father, John Adams, the sixth president did not employ enslaved people in the White House. Adams would later go on to become a leading voice of the abolition movement.

At that time, presidents were given a small allowance to run the White House. Extra expenses came out of the president's pocket. To save money, Jackson chose to bring enslaved people from his home to Washington. A year after Jackson arrived,

*The Coffin Handbill was an 1828 campaign poster entitled "An Account of the Bloody Deeds of General Jackson."* [Darlington Digital Library]

*Jackson's rowdy inauguration turned into a near riot when crowds of his supporters flocked to the White House.* [Library of Congress, Rare Book and Special Collections Division, 3a05553]

the 1830 U.S. census listed twenty-four people employed at the White House, most of them paid workers managed by steward Antoine Michel Giusta. They included Giusta's wife, maids, cooks, porters, gardeners, stablemen, and doormen. But that would soon change as Jackson settled in, reports White House historian William Seale. "By 1833 the hired staff was hardly more than one-third of the 1830 count, the balance being made up by slaves from the Hermitage."

The servants all wore specially designed uniforms, says Seale. "Like the other members of the household staff, those slaves who served wore the livery established for some time at the White House: blue coats with brass buttons, white shirts, and yellow or white breeches. Maids, who never appeared before the public, wore long dresses with long white aprons reaching to their ankles. All the slaves lived in the house."

According to Seale, the Hermitage servants, accustomed to simpler farm life, were overwhelmed when thousands of people descended on the White House to celebrate Jackson's inauguration. This occasion famously ended in a near riot as crowds swept into the White House for punch and ice cream, overturning tables in the frenzied rush.

"All of Jackson's servants were African American slaves who had worked under Mrs. Jackson's management probably for the better part of their lives," says Seale. "They were country folk."

There are few accounts of the Hermitage's enslaved people living in Washington. But some personal letters offer hints of life in Jackson's White House. Jackson's granddaughter noted that Jackson's personal attendant, George, always slept in the president's room with him. There is also mention of a carriage driver named Charles who was part of Jackson's White House "family." George, Charles, and at least one other enslaved man named John Fulton were trusted enough to serve as couriers, and they occasionally traveled alone back to the Hermitage with messages from Jackson.

The White House staff also included some free blacks, among them a young woman who worked as a pastry chef. During Jackson's second term, this woman asked Jackson's daughter-in-law, Sarah Yorke Jackson, if the president would purchase an entire enslaved family that included her sister Gracy. Sarah Jackson was acting as White House hostess, and Jackson agreed. He purchased Gracy, a seamstress, along with several other family members, from a Virginia man.

Andrew Jackson later "gave" Gracy to Sarah Jackson, and she became a baby nurse and personal maid to Sarah. The notion that a person could be a "gift" offends and boggles modern minds. But is this an example of Jackson's brand of kindness? Some historians see the gift as evidence of Jackson's desire to keep enslaved families together. After the Civil War, a woman who had been enslaved at the Hermitage told an interviewer, "They used to pick us up and sell us in those days, even little children not higher than your cane; but old master never did."

Jackson's eight years in office were marked by angry fights over such issues as a central bank for the United States (the forerunner of the modern Federal Reserve) and "states' rights," the idea that the individual American states retain certain powers and can ignore, or nullify, federal laws such as tariffs.

A firm believer in the Union, Jackson rejected the idea that states could secede for any reason. The tariff controversy was settled, but it hinted at a greater problem. The heart of the question was slavery and whether it would be limited by law as the growing nation added new states. Jackson himself predicted that "the negro, or slavery, question" would be the next great crisis.

Slave states did not want the United States government to place any limits on slavery. They also rejected plans to limit slavery in the new western territories as they gradually became states.

But the people who wanted to limit slavery in the western territories were becoming more powerful and starting to split the country along regional lines. Two political groups, the Liberty and Free Soil parties, emerged from this movement.

Even more divisive and controversial was the swelling chorus calling to completely outlaw American slavery. Abolitionists wanted not just to end the spread of slavery but to end it in America. The issue was becoming more than a noisy political argument.

What had once been a trickle of scattered voices grew into an angry stream. The waves of protest grew louder and more threatening. When a free black man named David Walker published a powerful pamphlet in 1829 called *Appeal to the Coloured Citizens of the World,* the raging flood threatened to break the dam. Walker called for enslaved people to openly rebel, in terms that shocked and outraged white America. He called for his "afflicted, degraded and slumbering brethren" to cast off their chains. Walker's defiant words warned that blacks would start to fight back and would be like "tigers and lions to deal with." He also said, "Believe this, that it is no more harm for you to kill a man, who is trying to kill you, than it is for you to take a drink of water when thirsty." His words were like a thunderclap. White Americans had never heard a black man speak so boldly before.

Enraged slaveholders were rumored to have put a price on his head. When David Walker died suddenly in August 1830, some believed that he had been poisoned. Most historians, however, contend that he died of tuberculosis.

In January 1831, another loud voice of abolition came ringing out of Massachusetts. In Boston, William Lloyd Garrison began to publish *The Liberator,* an abolitionist newspaper. Garrison called for immediate emancipation in language that left no room for compromise. In the first issue of *The Liberator* (January 1, 1831), Garrison wrote, "Let southern oppressors tremble—let their secret abettors tremble—let their northern apologists tremble—let all the enemies of the persecuted blacks tremble."

These were only words. But words soon became deadly acts. As abolitionist voices rose angrily, a murderous uprising shook

*Slaves are chained together as they march from the house of J. W. Neal & Co. in Washington, D.C. This illustration was printed on a broadside, or poster, during an 1835–36 abolitionist campaign to pressure Congress to end slavery in the nation's capital.* [Library of Congress, Rare Book and Special Collections Division, ppmsca-19705]

the nation. In 1831, a violent rebellion of slaves in Virginia led by Nat Turner made the threat of Walker's appeal a frightening reality. Turner's uprising left more than fifty-five whites dead. Anger and panic swept through slaveholding states.

There is no evidence that Nat Turner had read Walker's appeal, the writings of Garrison, or any abolitionist literature. But slaveholders blamed the violence on a "sinister Northern abolitionist plot to destroy their cherished way of life," as one historian put it. Americans knew the blood-soaked history of the Haitian revolution a few decades earlier. The idea that such a thing could happen in America was terrifying.

Along with the crescendo of angry writings and the real fear of more deadly uprisings, Congress was flooded with petitions aimed at ending slavery. One particular target was the slave trade in Washington, D.C., where auctions routinely took place within blocks of the Capitol and White House. Enslaved people sold there were marched through the city's streets in chains. Abolitionists began to produce broadsides—posters and pamphlets—that depicted slave trading taking place in the shadow of Congress and the White House.

Andrew Jackson was not a man who backed down from the assault on slavery. Old Hickory labeled abolitionists "monsters," called their writings "unconstitutional and wicked," and resolved to stamp out the abolition movement.

Jackson requested Congress pass a law to "prohibit, under severe penalties, the circulation in the Southern States, through the mail, of incendiary publications intended to instigate the slaves to insurrection."

This proposed ban included the pamphlets written by two women in South Carolina, heart of the slaveholding South. The Grimké sisters, Sarah Moore and Angelina Emily, were Quakers and daughters of a prominent South Carolina judge. They believed, as Angelina once wrote, "Man cannot rightfully

*Sarah Moore Grimké (left) and Angelina Emily Grimké (right) were outspoken abolitionist leaders.* [Library of Congress, Prints & Photographs Division, LC-USZ61-1608 and LC-USZ61-1609]

hold his fellow man as property." In response, slavery proponents in South Carolina made huge public bonfires and burned the abolitionist mailings of the Grimkés and others.

Jackson's request clearly trampled on the fundamental rights to free speech and a free press guaranteed in the Bill of Rights. But most people of the time didn't care. Abolitionists had few friends. Jackson had popular support against a group many Americans thought were troublemakers. In 1836, near the end of Jackson's second term, Congress adopted a gag rule that banned any discussion of petitions or legislation related to slavery.

More than fifteen years earlier, an aging Thomas Jefferson had said the dispute over slavery was like "a fire bell in the night . . . filled me with terror." Now, the flames of abolition were spreading and growing hotter, threatening a firestorm that could destroy the nation.

As these flames were stoked, Andrew Jackson had to deal with a real fire. In October 1834, a fire broke out at the Hermitage while President Jackson was in Washington. Jackson's beloved home was largely destroyed, and Andrew Jackson Jr., Jackson's adopted son, blamed servants for the disaster. "The cursed negroes were all so stupid & confused that nothing could be done until some white one came to their relief."

In fact, the fire started in a chimney and was accidental. Enslaved people had actually helped save the few furnishings that were spared. Jackson regretted the loss of his papers and furniture but quickly made plans to rebuild and restore the main house at the Hermitage, turning it into one of Tennessee's grandest residences.

The mansion's restoration was completed in 1837, the year that an aging and ailing Andrew Jackson returned to Tennessee. In Jackson's retirement, George remained his body servant, but Alfred became his constant companion during rides; that may have been one reason Andrew Jackson wanted to make sure Alfred was acquitted after the 1838 Christmas riot.

The enslaved family Jackson had purchased while in Washington also came back to the Hermitage with him. Among them

*The rear entry to the mansion at the Hermitage. This Greek revival mansion was a renovation and restoration of an earlier house that had been damaged by fire in 1834.* [Author's collection]

*Not far from the main house at the Hermitage stood Alfred Jackson's cabin.*
[Author's collection]

was the talented seamstress Gracy, who had nursed Sarah's children and been elevated to a supervisor of other household members. Seeing the ruffled shirts Gracy made for Andrew Jackson, a guest at the Hermitage wrote, "Her needlework was unexcelled."

In the fall of 1837, Gracy and Alfred were married. Their wedding suggests another strange picture of the intertwined lives of master and enslaved. Jackson's daughter-in-law, Sarah Jackson, took great interest in the event, according to accounts of the day. "She had the couple stand in the large hall while they were married and gave them a fine wedding supper. These two favorite servants were given a cabin near the house."

Alfred and Gracy lived in the rough log cabin, currently located in the work yard, a stone's throw from the rear entrance of the main house. A "double pen" cabin—two small square log rooms attached together—it was one story high, with low ceilings, rough wood floors, and few windows.

The cabin might have been physically close to Jackson's mansion, but it was a world away. Recent excavations at the Hermitage have uncovered evidence of as many as nineteen cabins, some of them smaller "single pens," one-room cabins. These archaeological digs have also turned up some 800,000 everyday objects including china, toys, and even amulets suggesting a connection to West African tribal religions and traditions.

A little more than a year after their wedding, Alfred was attending the ill-fated Christmas party where Frank was killed. After he was freed from the Nashville jail, Alfred returned to the Hermitage, where he and Gracy would spend the rest of their lives.

Andrew Jackson also spent the remaining years of his life at the Hermitage, with his adopted son Andrew Jackson Jr. and his wife, Sarah, riding every day with his granddaughter, Rachel. After he left office in 1837, the nation suffered through a serious economic depression. Jackson's financial health suffered as well, along with his physical health. By the late spring of 1845, now age seventy-eight, Jackson was in serious decline.

Years later, an aged Hannah would recall, "On Sunday, the day of his death, when I brought his egg and milk, he could not drink it. His eyes looked so curious that I went out and told Mistus Sarah. She ran to the storeroom, got some brandy, loaf sugar and spice and burned the brandy and carried it to him. He took one or two teaspoonfuls and it revived him, but he didn't speak the whole day."

Alfred was sent to Nashville to collect medicine and bring back a doctor. When he returned, Alfred saw other servants standing by the front window. "I knowed General Jackson was [worse]," he said. According to Alfred, someone suggested the servants leave, but Jackson said no.

Soon the entire household, enslaved and free, was standing beside Jackson's bedside. Jackson asked for his glasses, wet them with his tongue, wiped them on the sheet, put them on, and looked around.

Jackson asked, "Where's poor George and Hannah?"

George stepped forward, and the dying president asked him to remove two of the three pillows beneath his head.

According to Hannah, Jackson said, "I want all to prepare to meet me in heaven. . . . My conversation is for you all. Christ has no respect to color. . . . I am in God and God is in me."

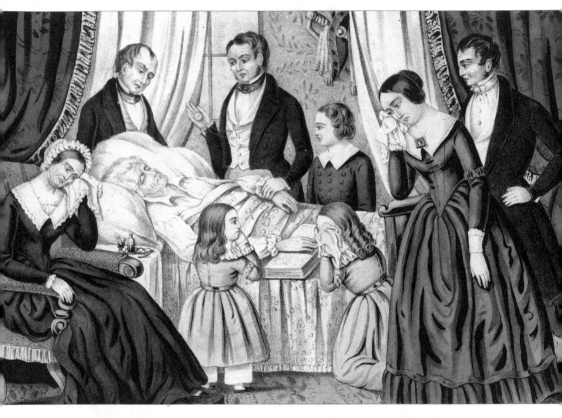

*This popular image of the day, entitled* The Death of General Andrew Jackson, *does not show the enslaved people who also attended Jackson at his death.*
[Andrew Jackson's Hermitage]

*The gravesite of Andrew and Rachel Jackson in the garden at the Hermitage.*
[Author's collection]

With that, Jackson hunched up his shoulders, took one breath, and, according to Hannah, "All was over. There was no struggle."

It was June 8, 1845.

Following Jackson's death, the Hermitage was taken over by Andrew Jackson Jr. and his wife, Sarah. They hired a tutor for their children, who once described an encounter with Alfred.

"Alfred was a man of powerful physique, and had the brains and executive powers of a major-general," the tutor recalled. "He was thoroughly reliable, and was fully and deservedly trusted in the management of plantation affairs."

Meeting Alfred one evening, the tutor found him looking gloomy. Alfred said, "You white folks have easy times, don't you? . . . You have liberty to come and go as you will."

The tutor suggested that everyone should be contented to do his duty and look to the next life in heaven, "where all inequalities would be made even."

Alfred then looked at the man and said,

"How would you like to be a slave?"

The tutor later wrote, "I have never yet found an answer to the argument embodied in that question."

When President Andrew Jackson died and his debts were paid, little was left besides the Hermitage property. Between mismanagement and the state of the economy, the farm suffered, and part was sold to the state of Tennessee with the intent of creating an old soldiers' hospital. Andrew Jackson Jr. and Sarah Yorke Jackson moved to Mississippi at the outbreak of the Civil War. Andrew Jr. died there from an infection after a shooting accident.

In 1862, when Nashville fell to Union forces in the Civil War, Union soldiers visited the Hermitage. Andrew Jackson was still an admired, larger-than-life president and war hero. In part out of respect for the former president, these troops never occupied the estate, which was still home to an enslaved community, some of whom had begun to escape the plantation. Others were being sold to raise cash. Alfred and Gracy remained.

When word of Lincoln's 1863 Emancipation Proclamation reached the Hermitage, all of the newly freed people were told they must legalize their marriages. Although Alfred and Gracy had been married since 1837, the couple remarried with an official license in 1866—just as Andrew and Rachel Jackson had once been forced to remarry.

Alfred took the last name Jackson after the war. He continued to farm the land now owned by Tennessee. With Jackson family finances ruined and most of the former enslaved community gone, the Hermitage soon fell into disrepair. Now old and poor, Andrew Jackson's daughter-in-law

Sarah was permitted to live at the Hermitage, relying upon Alfred and Gracy to care for her. She and Gracy both died there in 1887.

The Hermitage eventually became a public museum. Though he grew old, his memories remained sharp, and Alfred became the unofficial and much-sought-after tour guide. With Andrew Jackson's popularity undiminished after the Civil War, visitors flocked to the plantation to hear Alfred recount tales of life with the president. Alfred would talk for hours, as one account put it, and then expect to be paid a few coins. His tales of Jackson and the Battle of New Orleans would bring "showers of silver."

According to his listeners' accounts of Alfred's stories, Andrew Jackson was nothing less than a great general and one of the greatest presidents—a man with few equals. In the description of Alfred given in a 1915 book, the author said, "To him Gen. Andrew Jackson was the embodiment and concentration of all human grandness and nobility of character.... No general had ever achieved such victories. No President had ever equaled his hero."

Alfred continued to tell stories of Hermitage life almost till the day he died in September 1901. Born enslaved at the beginning of the nineteenth century, Alfred Jackson died a free man as the twentieth century began.

Carried from his cottage, his coffin lay in the main hall of the house, where he and Gracy had been married. Then Alfred Jackson was buried in the garden beside the tomb of Andrew Jackson and his wife, Rachel.

*The grave marker of Alfred Jackson, near the gravesite of Andrew and Rachel Jackson.* [Author's collection]

# SLAVERY IN AMERICA TIME LINE
## 1839–1850

**1839** The *Amistad* rebellion takes place when African captives on a Spanish slave ship overthrow and kill some of the crew. The ship is later captured in American waters. The Supreme Court orders the release of the captives, who have been defended by John Quincy Adams, saying that they are free persons.

**1840** The census counts 17,069,453 people in America; 2,874,000 are black; 2,487,355 of them enslaved.

**1841** The *Creole* rebellion takes place when a group of people being transported from Virginia to the slave market in New Orleans mutinies and captures the transport ship *Creole*. The mutineers sail to the British colony of Bahamas and are freed.

**1844**
- Outgoing President Tyler asks Congress to annex Texas.
- The gag rule is overturned in the House of Representatives.

**1845**
- Texas agrees to be annexed by the United States; to avoid conflict over that decision, President Polk negotiates with Mexico to buy its territories of Texas, New Mexico, and California. Mexico refuses.
- Florida is admitted as the twenty-seventh state, a slave state.
- Texas is admitted as the twenty-eighth state, a slave state, even though Mexico still claims Texas as its territory.
- Formerly enslaved, Frederick Douglass publishes his autobiography, *The Narrative of the Life of Frederick Douglass, an American Slave*. He becomes internationally known as a speaker and writer and is one of the most powerful voices of the abolitionist cause.

# "THAT ALL MAY BE FREE"

**1846**
- In May, Congress declares war on Mexico.
- About thirty Americans in Sonoma, California, declare an independent republic, breaking away from Mexico's control.
- Iowa becomes the twenty-ninth state, a free state.
- New Jersey abolishes slavery.

**1847**
In Rochester, New York, Frederick Douglass begins publication of his abolitionist journal, *The North Star*.

**1848**
- A peace treaty ends the war with Mexico. The United States receives more than 500,000 square miles of land.
- Wisconsin, a free state, becomes the thirtieth state.
- An antislavery coalition forms the Free Soil party and nominates former president Martin Van Buren as its candidate. Once sympathetic to slaveholders, Van Buren is not an abolitionist but joins those who oppose slavery's expansion in favor of free, white workers.
- Mexican War hero Zachary Taylor is elected president. A slaveholder from Virginia, he is the last president to bring enslaved people to the White House as servants.

**1850**
- President Zachary Taylor dies in office and is succeeded by Millard Fillmore, a New Yorker with moderate antislavery views.
- Congress passes five measures known as the Compromise of 1850, which Fillmore signs into law:
    - California is admitted as the thirty-first state, a free state.
    - New Mexico and Utah are organized as territories with no restrictions on slavery.
    - The boundaries of Texas are set without restrictions on slavery, and the U.S. government takes responsibility for Texas's debt.
    - The slave trade, but not slavery itself, is abolished in Washington, D.C., after January 1851.
    - The Fugitive Slave Act adds new rules for stricter federal enforcement of the Fugitive Slave Act of 1793. The law leads to angry protests and inspires Harriet Beecher Stowe to write a serialized novel that will become *Uncle Tom's Cabin*.
- The 1850 U.S. census counts 23,191,876 people; the black population is 3,638,808; 3,204,313 of them are enslaved.

There is not a nation on the earth guilty of practices more shocking and bloody than are the people of the United States, at this very hour.
—FREDERICK DOUGLASS, JULY 5, 1852

Seven years after the death of Andrew Jackson—the last surviving president to have taken part in the American Revolution—Frederick Douglass was asked to give a speech to mark the seventy-sixth anniversary of the Declaration of Independence in 1852.

Douglass had escaped slavery to become the most famous African American man in America. Large crowds flocked to his exciting speeches, in which he vividly told the story of his early life in bondage and escape from the cruelty he had known.

Frederick Augustus Washington Bailey was born enslaved in Maryland, around February 1818. He made his escape from Baltimore in September 1838. As a young man, he was a victim of the degradation of life in shackles. With some help from a sympathetic mistress, he taught himself to read. Hired out to work in a Maryland shipyard, he planned to flee with the help of Anna Murray, a free black woman. She provided money, papers that identified him as a free sailor, and a uniform. Arriving on New York's free soil, he later wrote, "A new world burst upon my agitated vision."

In New York, Douglass met David Ruggles, an African American abolitionist fighting against kidnappers who seized free blacks and sold them into slavery. That was the harrowing story recounted in *Twelve Years a Slave*, Solomon Northup's 1853 memoir made famous again by an award-winning film in 2013.

David Ruggles told Frederick and his new bride, Anna Murray—they were married in Ruggles's parlor—to head north to New Bedford, Massachusetts, a haven for freed blacks. Taking this advice, Frederick and Anna moved there, and he changed their last name to Douglass, which came from a famous poem by Walter Scott and was suggested by an abolitionist friend.

One night, abolitionist leader William Lloyd Garrison heard Douglass tell his story to a rapt audience. Taken by his rousing speaking style and electrifying presence, Garrison immediately enlisted Douglass as a lecturer. While on the abolition speaking circuit, Douglass's fame grew, and in 1845, he published his first of three works of autobiography, *Narrative of the Life of Frederick Douglass, an American Slave*. Douglass went on to produce an abolitionist news-paper, *The North Star,* and trav-eled to Europe to lecture on the antislavery cause. He feared that once he returned to America, he could be forced back into bondage under the 1850 Fugitive Slave Act. But he returned, defiant.

On July 5, 1852, Doug-lass gave a speech to com-memorate Independence Day. Perhaps expecting a patriotic speech celebrat-

*A retouched portrait of Frederick Douglass originally taken around 1850.*
[National Portrait Gallery]

ing the Founders, liberty, and equality, the audience in Roch-ester, New York, got something they hadn't bargained for—the bitter and biting oratory of a man who asked them, "What, to the American slave, is your 4th of July? I answer; a day that reveals to him, more than all other days in the year, the gross injustice and cruelty to which he is the constant victim."

He angrily denounced the patriotic holiday. "This Fourth of July is *yours,* not *mine. You* may rejoice, I must mourn. . . . There is not a nation on the earth guilty of practices more shocking and bloody than are the people of the United States, at this very hour."

The story of Frederick Douglass, who emerged as the most powerful voice of enslaved masses in the nineteenth century, is unlike the stories of the millions of other people who were brought from Africa in shackles or born into a life of slavery in America.

So are the stories of the five Americans in this book, as well as Sally Hemings and her children.

First, we know their names, just as we know the name of Frederick Douglass. That alone sets them apart from the nameless millions.

Second, because they lived with some of the most powerful and famous people in American history—and got to tell at least parts of their stories—these five experienced a world very different from that of the millions of people forced into labor.

But there is another crucial distinction. Like Frederick Douglass, these five people lived out their final years as free people. They did not end their days trapped hopelessly in the inhumane and brutal system of American slavery.

Ona Judge, the only one who escaped her captors, neither praised nor severely damned George and Martha Washington. By their own accounts and those of other witnesses, Billy Lee,

Isaac Granger, Paul Jennings, and Alfred Jackson had only good words for the people who had "owned" them. Perhaps they truly felt some kinship to the men who held the power of life and death over them. Maybe living in the shadow of these great men made them feel honored and special. Or maybe these emancipated black men were just telling their listeners, especially the white ones, things they wanted to hear. It would have taken a very brave—or foolish—black man to criticize four of America's most beloved heroes.

For many years, admiring biographers and historians either ignored or hid the relationships of these presidents to their slaves. Some apologetically argued that Washington and the other Founders who owned slaves were merely doing what was normal in their times. That is too easy a pass to hand out.

Once it was simple to praise these men and their heroic achievements in painting a picture of American pride and patriotism. Now it would be equally simple to condemn them for taking part in what can only be called a massive and long-lasting crime against humanity, and to call them hypocrites and negate all they did because of their roles as slaveholders. They bought and sold human beings—for profit and punishment. They paid men to hunt runaways. They ordered whippings—even if they didn't raise a lash themselves. These are deeply disturbing flaws that don't show up on the marble statues that honor these men.

But history is never a simple tale told in black and white. The story of these presidents and their connection to slavery is a complicated one. At times, some of them agonized over the great gulf between their words, ideals, and actions. Over time, some of their views and behavior changed, though never enough to make a difference to the many victims of slavery's colossal injustice. As we look back at the past, we must take these hard, cold facts into account.

The stories of these five people are exceptional. They help us to peel back some of the layers of legend and hero worship that obscure the whole story of American history. Each one of these five people demonstrated so many of the characteristics we admire in our historical heroes: resilience, sacrifice, loyalty, perseverance, faith, and, most of all, courage in the face of extraordinary challenges and seemingly impossible obstacles. In America, poems are written, portraits painted, and statues built to honor such people.

There are no poems or statues that recognize William Lee, Ona Judge, Isaac Granger, Paul Jennings, and Alfred Jackson. Perhaps the best we can do is shine a light on their stories to bring them out of the shadows of history and of the men who "owned" them. Through their stories, their voices, and a handful of images, we can recognize that they and all the millions they stand for were also "endowed by their Creator with the unalienable rights to Life, Liberty and the pursuit of Happiness."

That magnificent dream is what is truly exceptional about America. And the struggle to make it come true for everyone never ends.

# SOURCE NOTES

## INTRODUCTION

xiv  "the white man's power to enslave": Frederick Douglass, *Narrative of the Life of Frederick Douglass, an American Slave* (Boston, 1845), pp. 33–34.


## CHAPTER ONE

3  "The time is now near at hand": George Washington, "General Orders," July 2, 1776, in *The Papers of George Washington*, Revolutionary War Series, ed. Philander D. Chase, vol. 5 (Charlottesville: University of Virginia Press, 1993), pp. 179–182.

4  George Washington had teeth yanked: Henry Wiencek, *An Imperfect God*, p. 112.

4  Washington paid for nine teeth: Mount Vernon Ladies Association, "The Trouble with Teeth," 2015, George Washington's Mount Vernon, mountvernon.org; also Ron Chernow, *Washington: A Life*, p. 439.

7  the word *mulatto*: Annette Gordon-Reed, *The Hemingses of Monticello*, pp. 47–48.

9  "general inconveniency of living without them": Alan Taylor, *The Internal Enemy*, p. 36.

10  Philip Schuyler, a patriot leader: Ron Chernow, *Alexander Hamilton* (New York: Penguin, 2004), p. 210.

11  "The individual who refuses to defend": Andrew Jackson, "Proclamation to Louisianans," Sept. 21, 1814, in James Parton, *Life of Andrew Jackson*, vol. 1 (New York, 1860), p. 612.


## CHAPTER TWO

17  "If slavery be wrong": Charles Pinckney, in James Madison, *Notes of Debates in the Federal Convention 1787*, p. 505; also in Edward E. Baptist, *The Half Has Never Been Told*, p. 10.

18  "One day, when all our people": Olaudah Equiano, *The Interesting Narrative of the Life of Olaudah Equiano, or Gustavus Vassa, the African*, London 1789, ch. 2, e-book from Project Gutenberg, gutenberg.org

22  During the long voyage: Marcus Rediker, *The Slave Ship: A Human History*, p. 58.

26  "Along the dreadful way": Rediker, p. 5.

26  "If slavery be wrong": Pinckney in Madison, *Notes of Debates*, also in Baptist, p. 10.

29  This priest, Bartolomé de las Casas: David Brion Davis, *Inhuman Bondage*, p. 98.

30  Recent research suggests: Lisa Rein, "Mystery of Va.'s First Slaves Is Unlocked 400 Years Later," *Washington Post*, Sept. 3, 2006.

## CHAPTER THREE

37 "I hope it will not be conceived": George Washington to Robert Morris, April 12, 1786, *The Papers of George Washington*, Confederation Series, vol. 4, ed. W. W. Abbot (Charlottesville: University of Virginia Press, 1995), pp. 15–17.

39 brush his hair, and tie it back: George Washington Parke Custis, *Recollections and Private Memoirs of Washington* (New York, 1860), p. 163.

42 "any property obviously belonging": "Articles of Capitulation," Oct. 18, 1781, Avalon Project, Yale University Law School, avalon.law.yale.edu.

44 "Since you still have one hand free": Mary V. Thompson, "'I Never See That Man Laugh to Show His Teeth': Relationships Between Blacks and Whites in Washington's Mount Vernon," unpublished research paper, Mount Vernon, quoted in Wiencek, *An Imperfect God*, p. 120.

48 "By far the larger part of the slaves": Frederick Douglass, *Narrative of the Life of Frederick Douglass* (Boston, 1845), p. 13.

48 Family stories described Billy: Chernow, *Washington*, p. 118.

48 servants in British-style livery: Marfé Ferguson Delano, *Master George's People*, p. 19.

49 "The first difference which strikes us": Thomas Jefferson, "Notes on Virginia," in *The Life and Selected Writings*, p. 238.

49 an estimated 5 percent of Virginia's enslaved: Philip D. Morgan and Michael L. Nicholls, "Slave Flight: Mount Vernon, Virginia, and the Wider Atlantic World," in *George Washington's South*, eds. Tamara Harvey and Greg O'Brien (Gainesville: University Press of Florida, 2004), p. 212.

49 "I noticed one small boy": Louis-Philippe, *Diary of My Travels in America*, trans. Stephen Becker (New York: Random House, 1977), in Marfé Ferguson Delano, *Master George's People*, p. 22.

50 "the most polite and accomplished of all butlers": Custis, *Recollections and Private Memoirs of Washington*, p. 389, in Delano, p. 15.

51 "Will, the huntsman": Custis, p. 387.

51 "the best horseman of his age": Thomas Jefferson to Walter Jones, Jan. 2, 1814, *The Papers of Thomas Jefferson*, Retirement Series, vol. 7, ed. J. Jefferson Looney (Princeton, NJ: Princeton University Press, 2010), pp. 100–104.

51 Billy decided that black foxes: Chernow, *Washington*, p. 124.

53 These clothes were made: Wiencek, *An Imperfect God*, p. 123.

54 "We entered one of the huts": Julian Ursyn Niemcewicz, *Under Their Vine and Fig Tree: Travels through America in 1797-1799, 1805 with Some Further Account of Life in New Jersey*, trans. and ed. Metchie J. E. Budka (Elizabeth, NJ: Grassman, 1965), p. 100, in Albert Marrin, *George Washington and the Founding of a Nation* (New York: Dutton, 2001), p. 73.

56 "a celebrated artiste": Custis, *Recollections and Private Memoirs of Washington*, p. 422.

57 "Pattyrollers is a gang of white men": Charles Crawley, interview by Susie Byrd, 1937, *Born in Slavery: Slave Narratives from the Federal Writer's Project, 1936–1938*, Library of Congress, in Belinda Hurmence, *We Lived in a Little Cabin in the Yard*, p. 4.

SOURCE NOTES

58  "The two last of these Negroes": George Washington, "Reward for Runaway Slaves,"
    Aug. 11, 1761, in *Writings*, pp. 102–103.
58  One of them, Cupid, had been sick: Wiencek, *An Imperfect God*, p. 99.
59  "Let Abram get his deserts": George Washington to William Pearce, March 30, 1794,
    *The Papers of George Washington*, Presidential Series, vol. 15, ed. Christine Sternberg
    Patrick (Charlottesville: University of Virginia Press, 2009), in Wiencek, *An Imperfect
    God*, p. 125.
60  "With this Letter comes a Negro": George Washington to Joseph Thompson, July 2,
    1766, in *Writings*, p. 118.
60  "a Negro Girl named": Wiencek, *An Imperfect God*, pp. 180–181.
61  "fix the Shackles of Slavry": George Washington to George William Fairfax, June
    10–15, 1774, in *Writings*, p. 150.
63  "Unhappy it is": George Washington to George William Fairfax, May 31, 1775, in
    *Writings,* p. 164.
63  "If it will give Will": Lund Washington to George Washington, Dec. 30, 1775,
    typescript, Fred W. Smith National Library for the Study of George Washington,
    Mount Vernon.
64  "a thousand combatants were on the field": Israel Trask, in *The Revolution Remem-
    bered: Eyewitness Accounts of the War for Independence,* ed. John C. Dann (Chicago:
    University of Chicago Press, 1980), p. 408–409, in Chernow, *Washington,* p. 198.
65  "Washington frequently had Billy Lee": Chernow, *Washington,* p. 207.
68  "I cannot get as much cloth": George Washington to James Mease, April 17, 1778, *The
    Papers of George Washington*, Revolutionary War Series, vol. 14, ed. David R. Hoth
    (Charlottesville: University of Virginia Press, 2004), pp. 540–542, in Chernow,
    *Washington,* p. 325.
68  "The General and Billy": Martha Washington to Eleanor Calvert Custis, in
    Chernow, *Washington,* p. 360.
72  records show her receiving pay: *George Washington's Accounts of Expenses While
    Commander-in-Chief of the Continental Army, 1775–1783,* ed. John C. Fitzpatrick
    (Boston: Houghton Mifflin, 1917), pp. 23, 35–36, 53, 126, in Chernow, *Washington,*
    p. 394.
73  The two men stayed in the lavish home: Richard Beeman, *Plain Honest Men: The
    Making of the American Constitution* (New York: Random House, 2009), p. 35.
75  *Representatives and direct Taxes*: U.S. Constitution, Article I, Section 2, clause 3.
77  "No Person held to Service": U.S. Constitution, Article IV, Section 2, clause 3.
78  "The Migration or Importation": U.S. Constitution, Article I, Section 9, clause 1.
80  "as he could neither Walk": George Washington, April 22, 1785, *The Diaries of George
    Washington*, vol. 4, eds. Donald Jackson and Dorothy Twohig (Charlottesville:
    University of Virginia Press, 1978), p. 125.
80  Three years later, while on an errand: George Washington, March 1, 1788, *The
    Diaries of George Washington*, vol. 5 (1979), p. 281.
80  "he was now a cripple": Charles Willson Peale, 1804, *The Selected Papers of Charles*

*Willson Peale and His Family*, vol. 2, pt. 2, ed. Lillian B. Miller (New Haven, CT: Yale University Press, 1988), p. 696.

81  "Will appears to be": Tobias Lear to Clement Biddle, April 19, 1789, *The Papers of George Washington,* Presidential Series, vol. 2, ed. Dorothy Twohig (Charlottesville: University of Virginia Press, 1987), pp. 133n–134n.

81  He returned to Mount Vernon: George Augustine Washington to George Washington, August 20, 1790, *The Papers of George Washington*, Presidential Series, vol. 6, ed. Mark A. Mastromarino (Charlottesville: University of Virginia Press, 1996), p. 311.

82  As promised, after Washington died: Eugene E. Prussing, *The Estate of George Washington, Deceased* (Boston: Little, Brown, 1927), p. 159.

## CHAPTER FOUR

89  "I wanted to be free": Ona Judge cited in Henry Wiencek, *An Imperfect God,* p. 323.

92  Under the cover of night: Wiencek, *An Imperfect God*, p. 322.

95  "gratitude for the kindness": Martha Washington to Fanny Bassett Washington, May 24, 1795, in Wiencek, *An Imperfect God*, p. 325.

95  "The ingratitude of the girl": George Washington to Oliver Wolcott Jr., Sept. 1, 1796, Papers of George Washington, University of Virginia, in Wiencek, *An Imperfect God*, p. 325.

97  Martha Washington told her husband: Patricia Brady, *Martha Washington: An American Life*, p. 209.

97  "There is no doubt in this family": George Washington to Joseph Whipple, Nov. 28, 1796, Papers of George Washington, Univeristy of Virginia, in Wiencek, *An Imperfect God*, p. 328.

98  "Col. Washington appears at Congress": John Adams to Abigail Adams, May 29, 1775, *The Adams Papers*, Adams Family Correspondence, vol. 1, ed. Lyman H. Butterfield (Cambridge, MA: Harvard University Press, 1963), in Chernow, *Washington,* p. 183.

99  "Pieces of fabric cut": Brady, p. 152.

100  "perfect Mistress of her needle": George Washington to Oliver Wolcott Jr., Sept. 1, 1796, Papers of George Washington, University of Virginia, in Evelyn Gerson, "Runaway Slave Ona Judge Staines," 2000, Black History Stories, seacoastnh .com.

108  "would be benefitted by the change": George Washington to Tobias Lear, April 12, 1791, *The Papers of George Washington*, Presidential Series, vol. 8, ed. Mark A. Mastromarino (Charlottesville: University of Virginia Press, 1999), pp. 84–86.

110  "I wish to have it accomplished": Washington to Lear, April 12, 1791.

112  Ona was to be given to Eliza: Brady, p. 209.

113  "I wanted to be free, missis": Andrew Carroll, *Here Is Where*, p. 26.

114  Why was Whipple bargaining: Wiencek, *An Imperfect God*, p. 327.

114  "I do not mean . . . that such violent": George Washington to Joseph Whipple,

Nov. 28, 1796, Papers of George Washington, University of Virginia, in Wiencek, *An Imperfect God*, p. 330.

117 "Oh! Sir, I am very glad": Louis-Philippe, *Diary of My Travels in America*, in Delano, *Master George's People*, p. 31.

118 "They never troubled me any more": T. H. Adams, "Washington's Runaway Slave," *The Granite Freeman*, May 22, 1845.

118 "she did not feel as tho": Abigail Adams to Mary Cranch, December 1, 1800, as cited on mountvernon.org.

119 "I have recently made a visit": Rev. Benjamin Chase, letter to the editor, *The Liberator*, Jan. 1, 1847, in "1846 interview with Ona Judge Staines," The President's House Slavery, ushistory.org/presidentshouse/.

121 "No, I am free": Evelyn Gerson, "Runaway Slave Ona Judge Staines," 2000, Black History Stories, seacoastnh.com.

**CHAPTER FIVE**

125 "Nothing is more certainly written": Thomas Jefferson, *Autobiography*, Jan. 6, 1821, Papers of Thomas Jefferson, Retirement Series, Founders Online, National Archives, founders.archives.gov.

125 "One of the cannon-balls knocked": Isaac Jefferson, *Memoirs of a Monticello Slave*, p. 17–18.

127 "He's gone to the mountains": Isaac Jefferson, p. 19.

128 "Old Master had plenty": Isaac Jefferson, p. 19.

128 Many of the British troops found rum: Michael Kranish, *Flight from Monticello*, p. 193.

129 Young Isaac, his mother, his father: Isaac Jefferson, p. 21.

129 "put a cocked hat": Isaac Jefferson, p. 22.

133 "largest slave uprising in our history": Gary B. Nash, *Race and Revolution* (Lanham, MD: Rowman & Littlefield, 2001), p. 57.

136 "It was very sickly at York": Isaac Jefferson, p. 23.

136 "Wallis [General Cornwallis] had a cave dug": Isaac Jefferson, p. 23.

137 "General Washington brought all": Isaac Jefferson, p. 23.

138 Fifteen of them died of smallpox: Annette Gordon-Reed, *The Hemingses of Monticello*, p. 140.

138 "Jefferson sold several young men": Lucia Stanton, *"These Who Labor for My Happiness,"* p. 59.

138 there were 236,000 slaves in Virginia: Stanton, pp. 28–29.

140 Later, Campbell took Isaac: Ronald Roy Seagrave, *Jefferson's Isaac*, pp. 119–121.

140 "rather tall, of strong frame": Charles Campbell in Isaac Jefferson, p. 52, in Stanton, p. 130.

141 "shave, dress and follow me on horseback": Thomas Jefferson to Daniel L. Hylton, Feb. 5, 1792, *The Papers of Thomas Jefferson*, vol. 23, ed. Charles T. Cullen (Princeton, NJ: Princeton University Press, 1990), p. 102.

141 "to provide tips to other slaves": Stanton, p. 108.

142 "every one comes into the world": Thomas Jefferson, Howell legal argument, 1770, in Jon Meacham, *Thomas Jefferson: The Art of Power,* pp. 48–49.

142 "He is greatly addicted to drink": Thomas Jefferson, "Advertisement for a Runaway Slave," Sept. 7, 1769, *The Papers of Thomas Jefferson,* vol. 1, ed. Julian P. Boyd (Princeton, NJ: Princeton University Press, 1950), in Meacham, *Thomas Jefferson,* pp. 47–48.

142 Sandy was returned and sold: Stanton, p. 151.

145 "It is only through piercing the veil": Gordon-Reed, p. 85.

145 That same year, he recorded a census: Stanton, p. 4.

146 Patsy "recovered almost instantaneously": Thomas Jefferson to Thomas Mann Randolph Jr., Oct. 19, 1792, *The Papers of Thomas Jefferson,* vol. 24, ed. John Catanzariti (Princeton, NJ: Princeton University Press, 1990), in Stanton, p. 118.

146 "When he wanted anything": Isaac Jefferson, p. 27.

147 the "unpleasant contrast": Stanton, p. 20.

152 "A second working day began": Stanton, p. 21.

152 "My Old Master was as neat": Isaac Jefferson, p. 41.

153 "Mr. Jefferson always singing": Isaac Jefferson, p. 30.

153 "This miserable kind of existence": Thomas Jefferson to Elizabeth Wayles Eppes, Oct. 3, 1782, *The Papers of Thomas Jefferson,* vol. 6, ed. Julian P. Boyd (Princeton, NJ: Princeton University Press, 1952), in Meacham, *Thomas Jefferson,* p. 148.

155 Some historians believe that James: Stanton, p. 185.

155 "light colored and decidedly good looking": Harry S. Randall to James Parton, June 1, 1868, Papers of James Parton, Hougton Library, Harvard University, in Meacham, *Thomas Jefferson,* p. 217.

155 "Sally [was] mighty near white": Isaac Jefferson, p. 10.

156 "He trusted her": Meacham, *Thomas Jefferson,* p. 235.

159 Isaac set the standard: Stanton, p. 128.

162 They were among thirty enslaved people: Stanton, p. 129.

163 "Negroe conjurer": Thomas Mann Randolph to Thomas Jefferson, ca. April 19, 1800, *The Papers of Thomas Jefferson,* vol. 31, ed. Barbara B. Oberg (Princeton, NJ: Princeton University Press, 2004), p. 524.

163 Whether they died from their disease: Stanton, p. 130.

164 "At Washington I prefer white servants": Thomas Jefferson to John Wayles Eppes, Aug. 7, 1804, *The Papers of Thomas Jefferson,* vol. 31, in Stanton, p. 43.

165 "cruel war against human nature": Thomas Jefferson, "Jefferson's 'original Rough draught' of the Declaration of Independence," in *The Papers of Thomas Jefferson,* vol. 1, pp. 243–247.

## CHAPTER SIX

173 "A large part of his men": Paul Jennings, *A Colored Man's Reminiscences of James Madison,* pp. 7–8.

173 "The two races cannot co-exist": James Madison to Lafayette, November 1826, Papers of James Madison, Alderman Library, University of Virginia, in "Madison and Slavery," James Madison's Montpelier, montpelier.org.

174 "Mrs. Madison ordered dinner": Jennings, pp. 8–9.

176 "a boy under his mother's feet": Elizabeth Dowling Taylor, *A Slave in the White House*, p. 7.

176 "The east room was not finished": Jennings, pp. 5–6.

177 "On the 24th of August": Jennings, p. 8.

177 "Since sunrise I have been": Dolley Payne Todd Madison to Lucy Payne Washington Todd, Aug. 23, 1814, Dolley Payne Madison Papers, Library of Congress, in William Seale, *The President's House*, vol. 1, p. 130.

178 "As Sukey, the house-servant": Jennings, pp. 8–9.

178 Gathering "what silver she could": Jennings, p. 9.

180 Thousands took the chance: Alan Taylor, *The Internal Enemy*, p. 3.

181 "People were running": Jennings, p. 9.

182 "This is totally false": Jennings, p. 13.

185 "Several kinds of wine": Seale, p. 133.

185 "warmly recall Mrs. Madison's seat": Catherine Allgor, *A Perfect Union*, p. 316.

185 "I heard a tremendous explosion": Jennings, p. 11.

188 "We were crazy with joy": Jennings, pp. 13–14.

189 "I don't think he drank": Jennings, pp. 15–16.

192 "It is prudent such": James Madison to William Bradford, Nov. 26, 1774, *The Papers of James Madison*, vol. 1, eds. William T. Hutchinson and William M. E. Rachal (Chicago: University of Chicago Press, 1962), in Alan Taylor, *The Internal Enemy*, p. 23.

193 "He and Mr. Madison": Jennings, p. 17.

195 "The two races cannot co-exist: Madison to Lafayette, November 1826.

198 "Nothing more than a change": Jennings, p. 19.

198 "Mr. Madison, I think": Jennings, p. 15.

200 "Pore fanney": Paul Jennings to Sukey, May 13, 1844, in Elizabeth Dowling Taylor, *A Slave in the White House*, p. 151.

201 "I give to my mulatto man": Dolley Payne Todd Madison, Last Will and Testament, Feb. 1, 1841, Albert and Shirley Small Special Collections, University of Virginia.

201 According to an abolitionist newspaper: Elizabeth Dowling Taylor, p. 156.

201 "I have paid $120": Daniel Webster, March 19, 1847, in Elizabeth Dowling Taylor, p. 160.

202 Through a middleman: Elizabeth Dowling Taylor, p. 159.

202 "In the last days of her life": Jennings, pp. 14–15.

203 "Paul Jennings was one": Elizabeth Dowling Taylor, p. 165.

204 By 1848, Dolley Madison had sold: Elizabeth Dowling Taylor, p. 174.

205 "None did more valiant service": Elizabeth Dowling Taylor, p. 173.

206 Considered the first memoir: Elizabeth Dowling Taylor, p. 215.

207 Paul Jennings most likely would have: Elizabeth Dowling Taylor, p. 212.

## CHAPTER SEVEN

211  "Stop the Runaway": Andrew Jackson, advertisement, Sept. 26, 1804, *The Papers of Andrew Jackson*, Main Series, vol. 2, ed. Harold D. Moser (Knoxville: University of Tennessee Press, 1984), in Jon Meacham, *American Lion*, p. 303; also in Andrew Burstein, *The Passions of Andrew Jackson*, p. 24.

211  "You white folks have": Alfred Jackson in Roeliff Brinkerhoff, *Recollections of a Lifetime* (Cincinnati: Robert Clarke, 1900), p. 61.

212  "We didn't know but one holiday": Baily Cunningham in Belinda Hurmence, *We Lived in a Little Cabin in the Yard,* p. 11.

212  "cryed out he was the best man": Andrew Jackson to John A. Shute, Jan. 3, 1839, Andrew Jackson Papers, 1775–1874, Library of Congress, in Matthew Warshauer, "Andrew Jackson: Chivalric Slave Master," *Tennessee Historical Quarterly* 65, no. 3 (Fall 2006), p. 216.

214  "Frank picked up a bench": Andrew Jackson to John A. Shute, Jan. 3, 1839.

216  "One of these same dusky pickaninnies": Mary C. Dorris, *Preservation of the Hermitage 1889–1915* (Ladies' Hermitage Association, 1915), p. 122.

216  "when he was driving the carriage": Dorris, p. 123.

223  she would comb "ole master's hair": "Old Hannah: Reminiscences of the Hermitage," *Cincinnati Commercial*, June 22, 1880.

226  "the most roaring, rollicking, game-cocking": James Parton, *Life of Andrew Jackson,* vol. 1 (New York, 1860), p. 104, in Meacham, *American Lion*, p. 20.

230  "I am glad the old gentleman": Andrew Jackson in Burke Davis, *Old Hickory: A Life of Andrew Jackson* (New York: Dial Press, 1977), p. 149, in A. J. Langguth, *Union 1812*, p. 379.

230  "Once Jackson had secured victory": Gene Allen Smith, *The Slaves' Gamble*, p. 165.

231  "I can and do forgive": Andrew Jackson in Cyrus Townsend Brady, *The True Andrew Jackson* (Philadelphia: J. B. Lippincott, 1906), p. 176.

233  "a tall gaunt man, standing straight": Arthur M. Schlesinger Jr., *The Age of Jackson* (Boston: Little, Brown, 1945)*,* p. 6.

234  "By 1833 the hired staff": William Seale, *The President's House,* vol. 1, p. 178.

234  "Like the other members of the household staff": Seale, pp. 178–179.

235  "All of Jackson's servants were": Seale, p. 175.

235  Jackson's granddaughter noted: Warshauer, "Andrew Jackson: Chivalric Slave Master," p. 215.

236  "They used to pick us up": "Old Hannah: Reminiscences of the Hermitage," *Cincinnati Commercial*, June 22, 1880.

237  "the negro, or slavery, question": Andrew Jackson to Andrew I. Crawford, May 1, 1833, Abraham Lincoln Papers, Library of Congress, in H. W. Brands, *Andrew Jackson,* p. 539.

238  "afflicted, degraded and slumbering brethren": David Walker, *Appeal to the Coloured Citizens of the World,* pp. 27–28.

238  When David Walker died suddenly: Sean Wilentz, *The Rise of American Democracy: Jefferson to Lincoln* (New York: W. W. Norton, 2005), p. 330.

240 "sinister Northern abolitionist plot": Stephen B. Oates, *The Fires of Jubilee*, p. 129.
241 "prohibit, under severe penalties": Andrew Jackson, "Seventh Annual Message," December 7, 1835, in *A Compilation of the Messages and Papers of the Presidents*, vol. 3, ed. James D. Richardson (New York, 1897), p. 1395, in Meacham, *American Lion*, p. 305.
241 "Man cannot rightfully hold": A. E. Grimké to Catherine E. Beecher, June 12, 1837, in *Letters to Catherine E. Beecher* (Boston, 1838), p. 4.
242 "a fire bell in the night": Thomas Jefferson to John Holmes, April 22, 1820, Papers of Thomas Jefferson, Retirement Series, Founders Online, National Archives, founders.archives.gov.
242 "The cursed negroes": Andrew Jackson Jr. in Robert V. Remini, *The Course of American Democracy, 1833–1845*, vol. 3 of *Andrew Jackson* (Baltimore: Johns Hopkins University Press, 1984), p. 185.
244 "She had the couple stand": Dorris, *Preservation of the Hermitage*, p. 125, in Warshauer, p. 221.
246 "I knowed General Jackson": Dorris, p. 139.
246 "I want all to prepare": The deathbed scene is told in "Old Hannah: Reminiscences of the Hermitage," *Cincinnati Commercial*, June 22, 1880.
249 "Alfred was a man of powerful physique": The tutor, Roeliff Brinkerhoff, recounted his conversation with Alfred in his book, *Recollections of a Lifetime* (Cincinnati: Robert Clarke, 1900), pp. 60–61, which is cited in Meacham, *American Lion*, pp. 303–304.
251 "To him Gen. Andrew Jackson": Dorris, p. 119.

## AFTERWORD
259 "What, to the American slave": Frederick Douglass, "The Meaning of July Fourth for the Negro," in *The Life and Writings of Frederick Douglass*, vol. 2, ed. Philip S. Foner (New York: International Publishers, 1950), reprinted online in "Africans in America," pbs.org.

# BIBLIOGRAPHY

Allgor, Catherine. *A Perfect Union: Dolley Madison and the Creation of the American Nation*. New York: Holt, 2006.

———. *Dolley Madison: The Problem of National Unity*. Boulder, CO: Westview Press, 2013.

Baptist, Edward E. *The Half Has Never Been Told: Slavery and the Making of American Capitalism*. New York: Basic Books, 2014.

Berlin, Ira. *Many Thousands Gone: The First Two Centuries of Slavery in North America*. Cambridge, MA: Belknap/Harvard University Press, 1998.

Blight, David W. *A Slave No More: Two Men Who Escaped to Freedom*. Orlando, FL: Houghton Mifflin Harcourt, 2007.

Brady, Patricia. *Martha Washington: An American Life*. New York: Viking, 2005.

Brands, H. W. *Andrew Jackson: His Life and Times*. New York: Doubleday, 2005.

Brookhiser, Richard. *James Madison*. New York: Basic Books, 2011.

Burstein, Andrew. *The Passions of Andrew Jackson*. New York: Knopf, 2003.

Carroll, Andrew. *Here Is Where: Discovering America's Great Forgotten History*. New York: Crown, 2013.

Cheney, Lynne. *James Madison: A Life Reconsidered*. New York: Viking, 2014.

Chernow, Ron. *Washington: A Life*. New York: Penguin, 2010.

Davis, David Brion. *Inhuman Bondage: The Rise and Fall of Slavery in the New World*. Oxford: Oxford University Press, 2006.

———. *The Problem of Slavery in the Age of Emancipation*. New York: Knopf, 2014.

———. *The Problem of Slavery in the Age of Revolution: 1770–1823*. Oxford: Oxford University Press, 1999.

Delano, Marfé Ferguson. *Master George's People: George Washington, His Slaves, and His Revolutionary Transformation*. Washington, D.C.: National Geographic Society, 2013.

Ellis, Joseph J. *American Sphinx: The Character of Thomas Jefferson*. New York: Knopf, 1996.

Fleming, Thomas. *Washington's Secret War: The Hidden History of Valley Forge*. New York: HarperCollins, 2005.

Foner, Eric. *Gateway to Freedom: The Hidden History of the Underground Railroad.* New York: Norton, 2015.

Franklin, John Hope, and Alfred A. Moss Jr. *From Slavery to Freedom: A History of African Americans,* 8th ed. New York: Knopf, 2000.

Goldberg, Vicki. *The White House: The President's Home in Photographs and History.* In cooperation with the White House Historical Association. New York: Little, Brown, 2011.

Gordon-Reed, Annette. *The Hemingses of Monticello: An American Family.* New York: Norton, 2008.

Hofstadter, Richard. *America at 1750: A Social Portrait.* New York: Knopf, 1971.

Howe, Daniel Walker. *What Hath God Wrought: The Transformation of America, 1815–1848.* Oxford: Oxford University Press, 2007.

Hurmence, Belinda, ed. *We Lived in a Little Cabin in the Yard.* Winston-Salem, NC: John F. Blair, 1994.

Jefferson, Isaac. *Memoirs of a Monticello Slave: As Dictated to Charles Campbell in the 1840's by Isaac, One of Thomas Jefferson's Slaves.* Charlottesville: University of Virginia Press, 1951.

Jefferson, Thomas. *The Life and Selected Writings of Thomas Jefferson.* Edited by Adrienne Koch and William Peden. New York: Modern Library, 1998.

———. *Public and Private Papers by Thomas Jefferson.* Edited by Merrill D. Peterson. New York: Vintage Books/Library of America, 1990.

Jennings, Paul. *A Colored Man's Reminiscences of James Madison.* Facsimile of first edition. Orange, VA: The Montpelier Foundation, 2010.

Klein, Herbert S. *The Atlantic Slave Trade.* Cambridge: Cambridge University Press, 1999.

Kolchin, Peter. *American Slavery: 1619–1877.* New York: Hill and Wang, 1993.

Kranish, Michael. *Flight from Monticello: Thomas Jefferson at War.* Oxford: Oxford University Press, 2010.

Langguth, A. J. *Union 1812: The Americans Who Fought the Second War of Independence.* New York: Simon & Schuster, 2006.

Larson, Edward J., and Michael P. Winship. *The Constitutional Convention: A Narrative History from the Notes of James Madison.* New York: Modern Library, 2005.

Lusane, Clarence. *The Black History of the White House.* San Francisco: City Lights Books, 2011.

Madison, Dolley Payne. *The Selected Letters of Dolley Payne Madison.* Edited by David B. Mattern and Holly C. Shulman. Charlottesville: University of Virginia Press, 2003.

Madison, James. *Notes of Debates in the Federal Convention of 1787*. New York: Norton, 1987.

———. *Writings*. Edited by Jack N. Rakove. New York: Library of America, 1999.

Mayer, Henry. *All on Fire: William Lloyd Garrison and the Abolition of Slavery*. New York: Norton, 1998.

Meacham, Jon. *American Lion: Andrew Jackson in the White House*. New York: Random House, 2008.

———. *Thomas Jefferson: The Art of Power*. New York: Random House, 2012.

Mellon, James, ed. *Bullwhip Days: The Slaves Remember*. New York: Grove Press, 1988.

Oates, Stephen B. *The Fires of Jubilee: Nat Turner's Fierce Rebellion*. New York: Harper & Row, 1975.

Rakove, Jack N. *James Madison and the Creation of the American Republic*. New York: Longman, 2002.

Rediker, Marcus. *The Slave Ship: A Human History*. New York: Viking, 2007.

Remini, Robert V. *Andrew Jackson*. New York: Twayne, 1966.

Reynolds, David S. *Waking Giant: America in the Age of Jackson*. New York: Harper, 2008.

Ricks, Mary Kay. *Escape on the Pearl: The Heroic Bid for Freedom on the Underground Railroad*. New York: Morrow, 2007.

Seagrave, Ronald Roy. *Jefferson's Isaac: From Monticello to Petersburg*. Denver: Outskirts Press, 2011.

Seale, William. *The President's House: A History*, vol. 1, 2nd ed. Baltimore: Johns Hopkins University Press, 2008.

Smith, Gene Allen. *The Slaves' Gamble: Choosing Sides in the War of 1812*. New York: Palgrave Macmillan, 2013.

Stanton, Lucia. *"Those Who Labor for My Happiness": Slavery at Thomas Jefferson's Monticello*. Charlottesville: University of Virginia Press, 2012.

Taylor, Alan. *The Internal Enemy: Slavery and War in Virginia, 1772–1832*. New York: Norton, 2013.

Taylor, Elizabeth Dowling. *A Slave in the White House: Paul Jennings and the Madisons*. New York: Palgrave Macmillan, 2012.

Walker, David. *David Walker's Appeal to the Coloured Citizens of the World*. Edited by Peter P. Hinks. University Park: Pennsylvania State University Press, 2000.

Washington, George. *Writings*. Edited by John Rhodehamel. New York: Library of America, 1997.

Wiencek, Henry. *An Imperfect God: George Washington, His Slaves, and the Creation of America*. New York: Farrar, Straus and Giroux, 2003.

———. *Master of the Mountain: Thomas Jefferson and His Slaves*. New York: Farrar, Straus and Giroux, 2012.

Wilkins, Roger. *Jefferson's Pillow: The Founding Fathers and the Dilemma of Black Patriotism*. Boston: Beacon Press, 2001.

Wills, Garry. *James Madison*. The American Presidents Series. New York: Holt, 2002.

———. *"Negro President": Jefferson and the Slave Power*. Boston: Houghton Mifflin, 2003.

# ACKNOWLEDGMENTS

The extremely gratifying and exciting work of researching and writing this book began with many visits over the years to the presidential homes of Washington, Jefferson, Madison, and Jackson. The book could not have been completed without the assistance and cooperation of the staff at each of these magnificent sites. I am especially grateful to Mary V. Thompson of Washington's Mount Vernon; Jillian Gale and Madeleine Rhondeau of Thomas Jefferson's Monticello; Christian Cotz, Meg Kennedy, and Rebecca Hagen of James Madison's Montpelier; and Martha Mullin and Ashley Bouknight of Andrew Jackson's Hermitage.

I would also like to thank Mary Alexander, representing the estate of the descendants of Paul Jennings, who emphasized to me: "At his death he [Jennings] owned two houses in Washington, D.C., and he lived his life as a free man, not bitter and angry toward his master's wife, but he supported her and cared for her until her death. . . . It is the determination and will to make one's life the best it can be, despite its beginning, that makes the difference."

The staff at the New York Public Library's Schomburg Center for Research in Black Culture and other branches of the New York Public Library also provided valuable assistance. And I thank Kerry Sautner of the National Constitution Center in Philadelphia.

I am also indebted to many other friends and colleagues who have been so supportive during my career and this effort, including Emily Brenner and Diane Burrowes. I am especially grateful to my agent, David Black, and his colleagues and staff: Susan Raihofer, Joy Tutela, Gary Morris, Sarah Smith, and Jennifer Herrera.

It has been a great pleasure to join the creative team at Henry Holt Books for Young Readers. For their enthusiasm, creativity, and hard work, I thank my editor, Sally Doherty, and her colleagues Laura Godwin, Jean Feiwel, Patrick Collins, Jennifer Healey, Johanna Kirby, John Nora, Rachel Murray, Allison Verost, Katie Halata, Kelsey Marrujo, and Meredith Pratt.

# ACKNOWLEDGMENTS

For their support and inspiration, I am always grateful to my son, Colin Davis, and daughter, Jenny Davis, who provided special expertise and insight on this subject and was an early reader of the manuscript. My wife, Joann, has been my steadying hand and partner whose encouragement, insights, and wisdom make my work possible.

# INDEX